The Sorceries and Scandals of Satan

Henry M. Tichenor

Tichenor at his desk reviewing an issue of his magazine.

To those in every part of the world,

who realize that the goblins of the

priests, and the governments

of the exploiters, are mere

Superstitions, this book

is fraternally

dedicated

The and &

Foreword by
R. Merciless

Sorceries
and Scandals of
Satan

By
HENRY M. TICHENOR

Author of *The Life and Exploits of Jehovah*,

The Creed of Constantine, etc.

Introduction © 2010 by R. Merciless
Cover and interior design © 2010 by Kevin I. Slaughter

ebook { ISBN-10: 0-9830314-2-8
ISBN-13: 978-0-9830314-2-0

paperback { ISBN-10: 0-9830314-0-1
ISBN-13: 978-0-9830314-0-6

hardback { ISBN-10: 0-9830314-1-X
ISBN-13: 978-0-9830314-1-3

First published in 1917 by Phillip Wagner,
Pontiac Building, St. Louis, Missouri.

This edition © 2010
UNDERWORLD AMUSEMENTS
www.UnderworldAmusements.com

Table of Contents

    Foreword 9

    The Sorceries and Scandals of Satan 27

    Prologue 33

1. The War that was Fought in Heaven 37
2. Satan Wanders the Earth 49
3. Some of Satan's Sinners and Jehovah's Saints 57
4. Satan and his Transformations 70
5. Our Inspired Insanity 86
6. The Wonders of Christianity 99
7. Enchantments, Transformations and Familiar Spirits 107
8. Where Did Satan Come From? 118
9. Satan's Sorceries in New England 128
10. Massachusetts Under the Rein of the Doctors of Delusion .. 142
11. From the Beast to the Human 168

    Works by Henry M. Tichenor 172

Foreword

The Historical Context of
The Sorceries and Scandals of Satan
and its Author, Henry M. Tichenor

by

R. Merciless

The book you hold in your hands is a rare gem of literary brilliance very nearly lost and forgotten by a world which today greatly needs to hear its message. This reprinting rescues this almost lost work.

It is a scandalous book. It dares to expose to withering examination one of mankind's most popular and beloved fantasies, the lie people love to hear and repeat to themselves, the brain poison to which they are inseparably addicted – that of organized religion, especially monotheism, and Christianity in particular.

It does so with all of the brilliant wit and sarcasm hinted at in its delicious title. Many pious Christians will no doubt snatch up this book on glancing the title, *The Sorceries and Scandals of Satan*, and assume it to be a work reinforcing their beloved priest's or minister's Sunday warnings about the temptations and snares perpetrated by a boogieman. It was perhaps at least in part for such an audience that the book was originally written nearly a century ago as a means to tempt them indeed to open their eyes to the silliness and unreason of the indoctrination promoted in their churches.

Despite its age, the text has lost little if any of its relevance in the near century since the work was originally published. This is due to the fact that in that same time, humanity has lost none of its propensity to remain mindlessly enchanted, enthralled and enslaved by religious dogma and its accompanying moralistic straitjackets. Likewise, vast swaths of the human race around the globe have been rendered utterly insane with murderous fanaticism to the point of lacking nearly all "humanity." Or, perhaps, as Nietzsche might have pointed out, they are all too human. Protestants kill Catholics in the name of religion in Northern Ireland. Orthodox Christians kill Muslims in Bosnia. Jews kill Muslims in the West Bank and Lebanon. And, Muslims kill Christians, Buddhists, Jews, African animists and seemingly anyone else earning their hatred in the name of Allah and jihad worldwide.

TICHENOR AND SOCIAL REFORM

The author of *The Sorceries and Scandals of Satan*, Henry M. Tichenor, was one of the more daring and incisive scribes articulating the passionate wake-up calls of the social reform movement in early twentieth century America. The moral and intellectual perspective of agents of change such as Tichenor was a continuation of the transformation in Western society which began conceptually and intellectually with the Enlightenment, was fanned into heated action in the American Revolution and over the next hundred years effectively unseated the old, inbred, enthroned, religion-protected monarchist tyrannies of Europe. It was a movement which recognized that the proclaimed divine right of kings and nobles to rule the masses was a lie and a fraud and that the established religious orthodoxies served to perpetuate that lie by pronouncing the kings as holy, encouraging subservience and masochism in the subject masses, and brainwashing them to believe that desire for knowledge or betterment (to say nothing of rebellion) was a sin sure to be avenged with eternal torment by an angry God. By the later half of the nineteenth century, the revolution had turned from ridding society of the tyranny of kings to liberating it from the capitalists born of the industrial revolution.

In today's oh-so-civilized employment environment of eight-hour workdays, five-day work weeks, labor laws, employee rights, and employer-provided health insurance, it is easy to forget that conditions were not always so. The era of the expendable worker virtually enslaved to a sweatshop or company town was a harsh reality against which the socialists fought. Today's workforce owes its protections, and indeed much of the modern economy and stable social order, to the advocacy of this progressive movement.

By the early twentieth century, the American aspect of the movement had matured to the point that the Socialist party was able to put forward a presidential candidate in the person of its leader, Eugene V. Debs, and to command measurable public support. Debs garnered close to a million votes (6% of the total) in the 1912 and 1920 elections. During this period the Socialist party elected two Members of Congress, more than 70 mayors, as well as many state legislators and city councilors.[i]

This movement spawned, and was in turn fed by, a rich literature of social commentary seeking to awaken the masses to their oppression, expose social institutions such as religion as implements of that oppression, and point out the illogic of the population's complicity in its continuation. This literature flowed from a vibrant socialist press including writers like Upton Sinclair, outlets such as the nationwide weekly newspaper *Appeal to Reason*, numerous newsletters, and publishers such as Haldemann-Julius and Phil Wagner. The *Appeal to Reason,* based in Girard, Kansas, had a circulation of 750,000 in 1913 making it one of the most widely read publications in the country and rivaling *The Wall Street Journal*.[ii]

---

i   Shannon, D. A. (1955). *The Socialist Party of America: a history*. Macmillan. p.5.
ii   Graham, J. (1990). *"Yours for the revolution": the Appeal to reason, 1895-1922*. Lincoln: University of Nebraska Press. p15.

Foreword

TICHENOR THE MAN

Few of the socialist movement's writers and editors, however, could match Henry M. Tichenor in his brilliant deconstruction of religious orthodoxy as poison to liberty and a tool of the capitalist exploiter. In the realm of opposition to religion, he has been ranked beside Clarence Darrow and Madalyn Murray O'Hair as a leading American freethinker of the twentieth century.[i] Consequently, the man and his works merit far greater attention than they have received.

Tichenor was born on October 23, 1858 in Orange, New Jersey to Stephen W. and Mary Elizabeth (Mulford) Tichenor. He was christened Harrison Mulford Tichenor but later changed his name to Henry.[ii]

Stephen Tichenor, the author's father, was a financially successful businessman and politician. In 1839, he moved to Texas where he owned and operated steamboats working between Galveston and other gulf and river ports. From there he moved on to California where he was successful in gold mining. After returning to New Jersey, he was twice the mayor of Orange and served as a lay judge under the appointment of George McClellan, the prominent former Civil War General, who served as Governor of New Jersey from 1878-1881.

Henry was educated by private tutors and at Adams and Prescott Military Academy in Orange. In 1878, at age 20, he launched a career in journalism as a reporter for the *Chicago Daily Tribune*. He married Zora Meredith of Fremont, Nebraska in 1886. They had two daughters: Laura and Mary. In 1894, he helped to establish the *Omaha Evening News* and in 1895 became assistant editor and later editor of the *Springfield Leader-Democrat* in Missouri.

---

[i] Brown, M. (1978). *Freethought in the United States: A Descriptive Bibliography*, Greenwood Press. p.69.

[ii] The National cyclopaedia of American biography. Volume 20 (1926). New York: J.T. White. p.82

In early life, Tichenor was strongly influenced by reading *Age of Reason*, the brilliant condemnation of organized religion authored by Thomas Paine, the firebrand Enlightenment pamphleteer whose *Common Sense* helped to inspire the American Revolution. Tichenor also conducted his own detailed study of the history of religion and of Marxist socialism. He became an ardent socialist and, as a conduit for the expression of his ideas, he began in December 1900 the publication of a magazine called *The New Dispensation* but the magazine had only a brief existence. Tichenor then worked for several years in the commercial world as a salesman, perhaps to better meet the financial demands of providing for a family.

TICHENOR'S EARLY WRITINGS

Around 1911, he began contributing occasional poems to *The National Rip-Saw*, "America's Greatest Socialist Monthly," edited by Phil Wagner. By the end of 1912 Tichenor had also published under Wagner at least five pamphlets including; "A Wave of Horror," "The Evils of Capitalism," "The Rip-Saw Mother Goose," "Woman Under Capitalism," and "Rip-Saw Socialism Songs."

In January 1913, while continuing to write for the *Rip-Saw*, Tichenor joined forces with Wagner's publishing company to launch his own socialist journal, *The Melting Pot*, a publication whose mission proclaimed in the inaugural issue was to subject to fiery scrutiny societies lies of class, privilege, war and most especially organized religion. The cover of the magazine carried an illustration of a metal worker with the tools of his trade and the motto, "If it won't stand the heat of the Melting Pot, its no good." Tichenor served as its editor until it ceased publication with his retirement in 1920. This venture was more successful than Tichenor's earlier failed publication, *The New Dispensation*. This may have been due to some improved marketing savvy gained through his years of commercial experience as a salesman. One ad gushed, "The Melting Pot – Have You Seen It? To read a copy is to become a lifelong subscriber."

In January 1914 Wagner and Tichenor visited Socialist party leader and former U.S. presidential candidate Eugene V. Debs and persuaded him to write editorials and to speak for *The National Rip-Saw*.[i] Later that same year, the *Rip-Saw* issued a collection of Tichenor's poems titled "Rhymes of the Revolution," including an introduction by Debs in which the prominent socialist heaped breathless praise upon the author: "He hates with a hate that is holy the brazen shams and superstitions inculcated by a mamonized church in the name of religion and scourges without mercy the pious perverts who under the cloak of the Carpenter betray their followers into bondage."

One of the included Tichenor poems was "My Religion."

> I care not for the harps and wings the preacher tells us of
> I care not for the songs he sings of mansions up above
> He cannot cast on me his spell and make me go plumb nuts,
> With pictures of his fabled hell, like he does some poor mutts;
> I do not want a creed that crams such nightmares in my head
> About a God that saves or damns the people when they're dead.
>
> I want Faith that takes the drone that lives on others' sweat,
> and drags him down from off his throne and tells the cuss to get—
> A Faith that drives the dogs of war back to the jungle den,
> and swears that butchers shall no more pollute the walks of men—
> A Faith that says that all the race are of one common blood—
> that smites oppression in the face and calls for brotherhood!

---

[i] Debs, E. V., & Constantine, J. R. (1995). *Gentle rebel: letters of Eugene V. Debs*. Urbana: University of Illinois Press. p.92.

 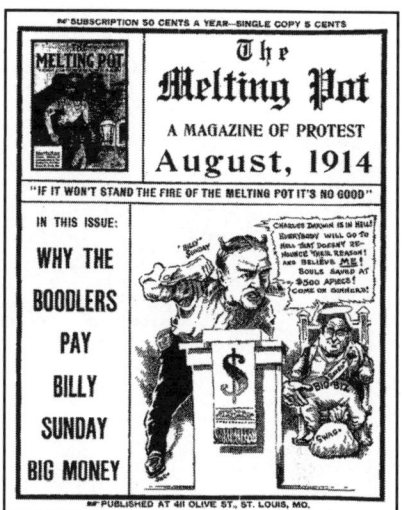

And when my bark at last shall sail to where the lovers rest,
this Faith alone, the Boatman Pale, will find upon my breast.

Another publication to which Tichenor contributed for *National Rip-Saw* in 1914 was a series of articles later republished as a 63-page pamphlet titled "Barnhill-Tichenor Debate on Socialism." Tichenor's opponent was John Basil Barnhill, editor of the monthly magazine *The American Anti-Socialist* and a veteran of more than 300 debates on the subject including a 1904 Chautauqua debate with Eugene Debs after his nomination for president. Along with the pointed indictments of Barnhill and folksy defenses of Tichenor, the publication included a handful of editorial-style cartoons. One of them depicted an evil, dark-faced Christian minister standing at a dollar-sign pulpit and exhorting a pious yet poor working-class family with "Slaves, be obedient to your masters!" as a fat, rich member of the "master class" looks on smugly.

Under Tichenor's editorship, *The Melting Pot* established itself as a scathing forum especially for attacking the scam of organized religion. The magazine soon set its sights on Billy Sunday, perhaps the most prominent evangelist in America and one particularly notable

for his lavish lifestyle. The front page of the August, 1914 issue of the *Melting Pot* featured a cartoon of Sunday, pockets bulging with money, again using a pulpit with a dollar sign, and preaching to a bloated character labeled "Big Biz." Tichenor said that he considered Billy Sunday and his peddling of hellfire and damnation fear for big money to be worse than "the dope dealers." The attack continued for several more issues. In February, 1915 a federal grand jury indicted Tichenor and Wagner on charges of circulating defamatory and scurrilous literature in the mails. A sympathetic judge fined the two only $100 plus court costs.[i]

In 2006, the Bank of Wisdom began selling a compact disc containing the first four years of the *Melting Pot;* issues published from 1913 to 1917.

TICHENOR IN MATURITY

The Melting Pot was only one of Tichenor's outlets. From 1913 until his death in 1922, Tichenor produced a torrent of social and religious commentary, including at least six books and twenty-eight pamphlets.

The tone and pace was set early with the August 1913 publication of the 63-page pamphlet, "The Roman Religion: A Short History of How the Holy Humbug was Hatched."

In 1915, Tichenor published his first full book-length work, *The Life and Exploits of Jehovah*, in which he brutally satirized the God of the Old Testament. This was followed the next year with *The Creed of Constantine; or the World Needs a New Religion* in which he turned his acid pen upon Christianity. Eugene Debs again wrote in support of Tichenor by producing a review of this book in the January 1917 issue of the *National Rip-Saw*.

The sting of Tichenor's attacks upon Christianity continued with the publication of this book, *The Sorceries and Scandals of Satan*, in 1917, and was followed by *Tales of Theology, Jehovah, Satan and the Christian Creed* in 1918, and *Mythologies, a Materialistic Interpretation: Analyzing the Class Character of Religion* in 1919.

In 1919, the *Appeal to Reason* newspaper was purchased by its editor, Emmanuel Haldeman-Julius, who used its printing plant to

---

[i] Bruns, R.A. (2002). *Preacher: Billy Sunday and Big-Time American Evangelism.* Champaign: University of Illinois Press. p. 194-195.

Published on the
15th of each month

Subscription 50c
a year

Single Copies 5c

Application made for
second-class mail at the
Post Office, St. Louis,
Mo.

The Melting Pot

Henry M. Tichenor, Editor

Phil. Wagner, Publisher

411 Olive Street
Saint Louis, Mo.

NO ORGANIZATION, POLITICAL OR RELIGIOUS, IS RESPONSIBLE FOR ANYTHING THAT GOES INTO THE MELTING POT.   PILE ALL YOUR CUSSIN' ON THE EDITOR

VOLUME 1   ST. LOUIS, MO., JANUARY, 1913   NUMBER 1

The Mission of The Melting Pot

TRUTH never needed a miracle to show it was the Truth. Truth is like fine gold—you can hammer it with a sledge hammer or fire it in the Melting Pot and it's still there with the goods when you've done your worst. But you want to be blamed careful how you monkey with a lie or you'll get it all out of shape. You can't rough-handle a lie—the thing won't stand for it. Hit a lie a sledge-hammer blow and it knocks it silly—fire it in the Melting Pot and it runs out like sewer gas. If you want a lie to hang together you've got to bandage it and bolster it and stand it up against a wall, and then hire a lot of liars to guard it. Common sense proves a Truth—it takes a canon law to make black look white. The Truth that two parallel lines can never meet needs no diet of holy men or popes' bulls to make you believe it. It's easy enough to understand that 2 x 2 make 4, but John Calvin, the inventor of the Calvinist creed, had to burn Dr. Servitus at the stake in order to make him believe that God Almighty had foreordained everlasting damnation for a large portion of the human race—and even then the doctor couldn't see it. Millions of victims have been thumb-screwed, racked, tortured, crucified and burned alive to keep a lie from looking too wabbly to suit the rulers and priests, and after all their tortures and murders it still takes an army of necromancers to nurse it. Truth stands serenely upon its own bottom, imperishable and eternal.

If the human race had chased after the Truth half as hard as they have after lies, we wouldn't be mussed up the way we are. For ages society has floundered along on hideous heaps of lies like a wrecked ship on the shoals. Catholic and Protestant, Jew and Mohammedan, have hated each other like wild beasts because of lies. All of them could easily agree on a simple Truth. Love is a Truth; hate is a lie. Peace is a Truth; war is a lie. Cleanliness is a Truth; filth is a lie. Brotherhood is a Truth; the king, the master, the slave, is a lie. Plain MAN and WOMAN is a Truth; the "Rev." Piousme and the "Hon." Billygoat is a lie. It takes bloody armies and butchering navies to keep a lie in running order; a little child could lead a whole world of Truth. A man clothed in a hickory shirt and pair of overalls can tell the Truth so that any sane person can grasp it; you have to rig him up in a long-tailed coat and a collar buttoned in the back of his neck so he can make you believe that something is so that isn't so.

Nobody would crawl on his knees to plain John Smith, dressed in an every-day suit of clothes. Decorate the cuss with purple robes and put rings on his fingers and a bejeweled bonnet on his noodle and John Smith becomes His Royal Highness the King. Plain John Smith was a Truth, just as Mother Nature made him. John Smith the King is a lie, and has to be decorated and besmeared all over, in order to make the befuddled people swallow him. When men and women shall open their souls and let the Truth flow in, it will be a beautiful world to live in; so long as they renounce their reason and follow after lies they are going to remain in a hell of a fix. "The Truth will set you free," and nothing else will. Our crowned and throned lies make us morally, ethically and religiously rotten. The New Society, that is on the way, wants nothing of the morals, ethics or dogmatic creeds of our present Roman-ruled world. William Liebnecht well said of the Socialists, "We will create our own morals and ethics, and we come bringing our religion with us."

To this end the Melting Pot will faithfully labor.

begin publishing a series of inexpensive, pocket-sized educational pamphlets designed to help elevate the poor, unschooled working classes by providing them with a means for cheap self-education. The pamphlets were about five inches high, less than 100 pages, and variously titled *Peoples Pocket Series*, *Ten-Cent Pocket Series*, or *Little Blue*

Books.ⁱ In retirement, from 1920 until his death in 1924, Tichenor produced at least 24 of these booklets, many on the subject of religion, beginning with a condensed version of Paine's *The Age of Reason* and including titles such as *Church History, Primitive Beliefs, When the Puritans Were in Power,* and *The Olympian Gods.*

The Sorceries and Scandals of Satan was written in the first half of 1917 at roughly the time of the entry of the United States into the bloody First World War. The extent of the carnage in the three-year-old conflict had already stunned the world. New technologies such as machine guns and poison gas combined with the disease-infested trenches to kill human beings on an unprecedented and horrifying scale. Over the course of the war, Britain, Germany and France saw 8%, 9% and 11% of their respective populations either killed or wounded. And for what? Many, like Tichenor, saw the war as a cynical invention designed to enrich the bankers and industrialists, and to entertain the princes and politicians with their favorite game – war and power – while serving only to lead the blind, patriotism-besotted masses to enormous slaughter. The influence of these historical circumstances echo with some frequency both directly and indirectly in *The Sorceries and Scandals of Satan.*

Tichenor's primary objective in this work was to reveal the hypocrisy of the Christian theologians and pulpit-pounders who attempt to strengthen their grip on the minds of the masses by linking the ills of the world with Satan, the proclaimed opposite of the purportedly good Jehovah which the clergymen claimed to represent. Yet Tichenor dares to show that the evils so frequently blamed on Satan, in fact, pale in comparison to the crimes, horrors and scandals perpetrated by both the God and the followers of Christianity. The hypocrisy and illogic of the preachers are thus laid bare. By revealing the rottenness at the core of the masses' beloved Christianity, he hopes to rip the blindfold from their eyes and liberate them from the

---

i   Degruson, G. (1990). "Little Blue Books" in Buhle, M. J., Buhle, P., & Georgakas, D. (Eds). Encyclopedia of the American left. New York: Garland. p.429

chains which have kept them enslaved through their own belief. The greatness of this work lies not only in the heroic nature of Tichenor's attempted rescue of humanity but also in the poetic beauty with which he renders it.

SATAN AS A LITERARY SYMBOL FOR FREEDOM AND REVOLT

One of the aspects of this work that makes it so important in intellectual and philosophical history is the manner in which Tichenor posits the mythical character of Satan as a heroic figure symbolic of knowledge, pleasure and liberty from human herd morality, and liberation from the cherished popular lies. Tichenor advanced this symbolism and polished it to a brilliance that had not been seen previously in America, but he did not invent it. The tradition of the symbolic literary and philosophical depiction of Satan as a positive, admirable and even exemplary hero can be traced back nearly five centuries to the epic poet John Milton.

Readers and critics have long recognized that the Satan character in Milton's *Paradise Lost* is, to the neutral modern-minded person, far more heroic and admirable character than the cold, obviously conceited Jehovah. To this day, scholars dispute whether Milton intentionally presented Satan in the more positive light or not.[i] Written between 1658 and 1664 on the heels of the English civil war in which the rebels of Milton's party had warred with and deposed but ultimately lost to monarchy, *Paradise Lost* is easily viewed as an allegory for Milton's own times and circumstances. Ostensibly he seems to be making amends with the re-established monarchy through a story in which the king of heaven defeats the rebel angels and their schemes. Yet Milton's lack of sincerity in such flattery and his love and respect for the rebel cannot be hidden. While his descriptions of

---

i   Forsyth, Neil. (2003). The satanic epic. Princeton, N.J.: Princeton University Press. p. 1-17.

God are flat and perfunctory, the poet pours forth the most beautiful and inspiring language to describe Lucifer's rebellious call to arms.

> Full Counsel must mature: Peace is despaired,
> For who can think Submission?
> War then, War open or understood must be resolved.
> He spake: and to confirm his words,
> out-flew Millions of flaming swords,
> drawn from the thighs of mighty Cherubim;
> the sudden blaze Far round illumin'd hell:
> highly they raged Against the Highest,
> and fierce with grasped arm's
> Clashed on their sounding shields the din of war,
> Hurling defiance toward the vault of Heav'n.[i]

This stunning positive depiction of Satan (either daring or subconscious) in *Paradise Lost* came at a pivotal point in human history. The irony is so thick. Milton ostensibly lauds the victory of Heaven's king but his style reveals something else. In the English Civil War, Milton himself had been aligned with the rebellion against the monarch. After the monarchy overcame the rebellion, Milton perhaps sought to gain enough favor to survive by publishing an analogous recounting of the legendary tale of Heaven's monarch overcoming Satanic rebels. In reality however, a deeper reading of the work reveals Milton's continuing alignment with the rebel cause. While both the anti-monarchists of the English Civil War and the literary character of Satan in *Paradise Lost* are defeated, in the longer-term both win ground. The power of both priests and kings in human affairs steadily declines from this point in history. The medieval mindset of the Dark Ages begins now to wane and the Enlightenment grows

---

[i] Milton, J., & Asimov, I. (1974). Asimov's annotated Paradise lost. New York: Doubleday. p. 48.

brighter. Mindless piety and mental slavery to either royalty or clergy begins to fade and the concept of the free individual begins to emerge. In the coming decades which follow Milton's work, these ideas spring forth to liberate humanity – or at least some of the literate, thinking minority – through the writings of Hume, Locke, Rousseau and Voltaire.

That the English elites began after this point to abandon actual belief in religion and rush to embrace pleasure and liberty with the idea of Satan as hero is demonstrated by the emergence of so-called Hellfire clubs. The Duke of Wharton established a deliciously decadent club by that very name in 1718.[i] A Dublin Hellfire Club was founded in 1735 by Richard Parsons, the First Earl of Rosse, meeting regularly at the Eagle Tavern on Cork Hill near Dublin Castle.[ii] Sir Francis Dashwood's "Monks of Medmenham" pagan revelry club of around 1750 was and is still informally referred to as a Hellfire club.[iii] In such a liberalizing social setting, the eccentric, iconoclastic poet William Blake could not only pen his own religion-upending works but also to recall with warm nostalgia the Satanism of his predecessor by noting famously that "the reason Milton wrote in fetters when he wrote of Angels and God, and at liberty when he wrote of Devils and Hell, is because he was a true poet and of the Devil's party without knowing it."[iv] Only a few decades after *Paradise Lost* was published, the playboy rakes of English society were laughingly and publicly embracing the character of Satan as an explicit heroic symbol for pleasure, indulgence and liberty from the suffocating,

---

[i] Blackett-Ord, M. (1982). Hell-fire Duke: the life of the Duke of Wharton. Windsor Forest, Berks: Kensal Press. p. 43.

[ii] Joyce, W. S. J. (1912). The neighbourhood of Dublin, its topography, antiquities and historical associations. Dublin: M.H. Gill. p.123

[iii] Ashe, G. (2000). The Hell-Fire Clubs: A History of Anti-Morality. Phoenix Mill: Sutton Publshing Limited. p. 111-131. See also generally Towers, E. (1986). Dashwood: the man and the myth. [England]: Crucible.

[iv] Schock, Peter A. (2003). Romantic Satanism: Myth and the Historical Moment in Blake, Shelley, and Byron. Palgrave Macmillan. p.48.

Foreword

institutionally-imposed morality being pushed like dope from the pulpits of Jehovah.

This Satanic symbolism, born in Milton's pen at the end of the seventeenth century and raised by the rakes of London in the eighteenth century now grew to full form in the nineteenth century, when Baudelaire and even earlier French poets dared to publish works which overtly praised and honored Satan and proclaimed him the hero of those who love freedom, reason and happiness. Priests and politicians were scandalized and horrified by such works. Revolutionaries, however, were inspired.

As early as 1846, the *avant garde* salon poets of Paris were sharing paeans lauding Satan as a heroic leader of justified rebellion. One anonymous bard of that year wrote:

> To thee, Satan, fair fallen angel,
> To whom fell the perilous honor
> Of struggling against an unjust rule,
> I offer myself wholly and forever,
> My mind, my senses, my heart, my love,
> And my dark verses in their corrupted beauty.[i]

In 1858, Pierre-Joseph Proudhon became perhaps the first true social revolutionary to employ Satan as a heroic personified symbol of rebellion and liberty.

> Come, Satan, come, slandered by priests and kings! Let me embrace you, let me clutch you to my breast! I have known you for a long time, and long have you known me. Your works, oh blessed one of my heart, are not always beautiful or good; but you alone give sense to the universe and prevent it from being absurd. What would justice

---

[i] Maigron, L. (1910). Le romantisme et les moeurs essai d'étude historique et sociale, D'après des documents inédits. Paris: Librairie Ancienne. p.187

Foreword

be without you? An instinct. Reason? A routine. Man? A beast. You alone animate labor and make it fertile; you ennoble wealth, serve as an excuse for authority, put the seal on virtue. Hope still, proscribed one! I have to serve you only a pen, but it is worth millions of bulletins.[i]

In the late 1860's, Giosue Carducci's poem "Hymn to Satan" lauded the Prince of Darkness as the symbolic champion of human pleasure and progress and was likely an anthem for republican forces of Italy overthrowing the secular influence of the Pope by force of arms.[ii]

Indeed, in the late 1870's anarchist Mikhail Bakunin wrote an entire book dedicated to exposing the explicit utility of the religion of Jehovah as a tool in oppressing and deluding the masses while recognizing Satan as the hero of human liberation. An extended section from his book, *God and the State*, is particularly worthy of examination:

> Jehovah, who of all the good gods adored by men was certainly the most jealous, the most vain, the most ferocious, the most unjust, the most bloodthirsty, the most despotic, and the most hostile to human dignity and liberty-Jehovah had just created Adam and Eve, to satisfy we know not what caprice; no doubt to while away his time, which must weigh heavy on his hands in his eternal egoistic solitude, or that he might have some new slaves. He generously placed at their disposal the whole earth, with all its fruits and animals, and set but a single limit to this complete enjoyment. He expressly forbade them from touching the fruit of the tree of knowledge. He wished, therefore, that

---

[i] Proudhon, P.-J. (1860). De la justice dans la révolution et dans l'église. Bruxelles: Office de Publicite., p.540

[ii] Merciless, R. (2000) "Giosue Carducci: 19th Century Poet, Statesman and Satanist", The Black Flame. Issue #16. Also http://www.churchofsatan.com/Pages/RMCarducci.html accessed on 5/29/08.

Foreword

man, destitute of all understanding of himself, should remain an eternal beast, ever on all-fours before the eternal God, his creator and his master. But here steps in Satan, the eternal rebel, the first freethinker and the emancipator of worlds. He makes man ashamed of his bestial ignorance and obedience; he emancipates him, stamps upon his brow the seal of liberty and humanity, in urging him to disobey and eat of the fruit of knowledge.

We know what followed. The good God, whose foresight, which is one of the divine faculties, should have warned him of what would happen, flew into a terrible and ridiculous rage; he cursed Satan, man, and the world created by himself, striking himself so to speak in his own creation, as children do when they get angry; and, not content with smiting our ancestors themselves, he cursed them in all the generations to come, innocent of the crime committed by their forefathers. Our Catholic and Protestant theologians look upon that as very profound and very just, precisely because it is monstrously iniquitous and absurd. Then, remembering that he was not only a God of vengeance and wrath, but also a God of love, after having tormented the existence of a few milliards of poor human beings and condemned them to an eternal hell, he took pity on the rest, and, to save them and reconcile his eternal and divine love with his eternal and divine anger, always greedy for victims and blood, he sent into the world, as an expiatory victim, his only son, that he might be killed by men. That is called the mystery of the Redemption, the basis of all the Christian religions. Still, if the divine Savior had saved the human world! But no; in the paradise promised by Christ, as we know, such being the formal announcement, the elect will number very few. The rest, the immense majority of the generations present and to come, will burn eternally in hell. In the meantime, to console us, God, ever just, ever good, hands over the earth to the government of the Napoleon Thirds, of the William Firsts, of the Ferdinands of Austria, and of the Alexanders of all the Russias.

Such are the absurd tales that are told and the monstrous doctrines that are taught, in the full light of the nineteenth century, in all the public schools of Europe, at the express command of the government. They call this civilizing the people! Is it not plain that all these governments are systematic poisoners, interested stupefies of the masses?

I have wandered from my subject, because anger gets hold of me whenever I think of the base and criminal means which they employ to keep the nations in perpetual slavery, undoubtedly that they may be the better able to fleece them. Of what consequence are the crimes of all the Tropmanns in the world compared with this crime of treason against humanity committed daily, in broad day, over the whole surface of the civilized world, by those who dare to call themselves the guardians and the fathers of the people? I return to the myth of original sin.

God admitted that Satan was right; he recognized that the devil did not deceive Adam and Eve in promising them knowledge and liberty as a reward for the act of disobedience which he bad induced them to commit; for, immediately they had eaten of the forbidden fruit, God himself said (see Bible): 'Behold, the man is become as one of the gods, to know good and evil; prevent him, therefore, from eating of the fruit of eternal life, lest he become immortal like Ourselves."

Let us disregard now the fabulous portion of this myth and consider its true meaning, which is very clear. Man has emancipated himself; he has separated himself from animality and constituted himself a man; he has begun his distinctively human history and development by an act of disobedience and science-that is, by rebellion and by thought.[i] This literary and philosophical tradition of linking the mythical character of Satan, the rebel angel, with the human struggle for freedom, liberty and self-determination likewise featured in George Bernard Shaw's 1897 play *"The Devil's Disciple"* in which the main character, Richard Dudgeon, a fearless and brutally just American Revolutionary war hero explicitly proclaims himself an overt Satanist:

> They call me the Devil's Disciple…Because it's true. I was brought up in the other service; but I knew from the start that the devil was my natural master and captain and friend. I saw that he was in the right, and that the world cringed to his conqueror only through fear. I prayed secretly to him; and he comforted me, and saved me from having my spirit broken in this house of children's tears. I promised him my soul, and swore an oath that I would stand up for him in this world and stand by him in the next. That promise and that oath made a man of me. From this day this house is his home; no child shall cry in it; this hearth is his altar; and no soul shall cower over it in the dark evening and be afraid.

The depiction of this linkage between Satan and liberty in a positive, heroic light had become at least somewhat publicly acceptable by this time. The production was so popular when it was staged in New York City that it became the first Shaw play to successfully earn a profit. It ran for 64 performances at the Fifth Avenue Theater,

---

i   Bakunin, M. A. (1900). *God and the State*. San Francisco: Free Society Library. Chapter 1. Also http://www.marxists.org/reference/archive/bakunin/works/godstate/ch01.htm accessed on 5/29/2008

grossing $50,000.[i] This equates to roughly $1.3 million in today's dollars.[ii]

Anatole France's 1914 novel, *The Revolt of the Angels*, tells the tale of a guardian angel who educates himself by reading books in an earthly library, abandons his heavenly master, and joins a group of Lucifer's demons plotting a renewed revolution. France is so comfortable with the positive and supportive depiction of satanic rebellion that he presents his story in an almost light-hearted tone.

Recalling his newspaper career contemporaneous with that of Tichenor shortly after the turn of the century, the iconoclastic American social commentator H.L. Mencken likewise wrapped himself in the Devil's banner in defense of liberty from moralistic tyrants. "I made up my mind at once that my true and natural allegiance was to the Devil's party, and it has been my firm belief ever since that all persons who devote themselves to forcing virtue on their fellow men deserve nothing better than kicks in the pants."[iii]

In 1971, radical social activist Saul Alinsky likewise gave a nod to this tradition in the opening pages of his still-influential work, Rules for Radicals, in which he wrote, "Lest we forget at least an over-the-shoulder acknowledgment to the very first radical: from all our legends, mythology, and history (and who is to know where mythology leaves off and history begins — or which is which), the first radical known to man who rebelled against the establishment and did it so effectively that he at least won his own kingdom — Lucifer."[iv]

---

i   Wilson, C. (1988), "How 'The Devil' Hauled Shaw Up From Hell," New York Times, Sunday, November 13, 1988, Section 2 page 5 of the New York edition. *See also* Wilson, C. (1969), Bernard Shaw: A Reassessment, Athenaeum.

ii Williamson, S. H. (2008) "Six Ways to Compute the Relative Value of a U.S. Dollar Amount, 1790 to Present," MeasuringWorth website http://www.measuringworth.com/uscompare/ accessed on 8/15/2009.

iii Mencken, H.L. (1941). *Newspaper Days: Mencken's Autobiography: 1899-1906.* New York: Knopf. p. 37

iv Alinsky, S. D. (1971). *Rules for radicals: A practical primer for realistic radicals.* New York: Random House. p. ix

It is to this long tradition of Satanic revolutionary literature that Tichenor's *The Sorceries and Scandals of Satan* makes such a valuable contribution – a tradition which, even if largely now absent from political philosophy, continues to this day in art, literature and even formalized albeit unorthodox religion in the form of today's Church of Satan established by Anton Szandor LaVey in 1966. LaVey's paradigm-shattering book, *The Satanic Bible*, has been in continuous publication since 1969 and still sells briskly.[i]

Even for those who are neither Satanists nor Socialists, Tichenor's *The Sorceries and Scandals of Satan* is an important artifact in the social history of America and indeed serves as a clarion call for all of humanity. As Tichenor articulates in its final paragraphs, his book stands as a small beacon of hope to guide humanity to a possible future of true individual happiness and freedom from the herd-like mental slavery of the world's tyrannical monotheistic religions.

---

[i] Amazon.com online sales ranking for this book by the deceased "Black Pope" accessed on 6/15/2008 was #10,270. In contrast, the sales ranking for the bestselling book by the recently deceased Catholic Pope, John Paul II was #62,193.

The Sorceries and Scandals of Satan

Prologue

The kind and beautiful gods and goddesses were discarded by the priests of Christianity; only the cruel and vindictive ones were preserved. Jehovah, with horns on his fingers and a sword in his jaws, was saved, while Apollo, charming and graceful, with the laurel crown upon his flowing hair, guardian deity of nine muses that filled the world with music and poetry, with the drama and the dance, with the liberal arts and sciences, was repudiated by the priests of sackcloth and ashes, of damnation and Hell. Venus, goddess of love and beauty, born of the froth of the sea and cradled in a shell of pearl, was denounced and dethroned, and a Holy Virgin, to whom love was a vice arid sex a sin, was made Queen of Heaven. The woodland Pan of milk and honey who played such sweet strains on his pipe of reeds that all creation was entranced, was forgotten, and a tortured Christ, slaughtered to appease the fury of the god that begat him, took his place. The jovial Bacchus, god of wine, adorned with leaves of ivy and grape, was cast aside, and a melancholy Holy Ghost, created in the image of a pigeon, made men miserable. Charon, boatman of departed souls, always waiting on the shore of the sea of Avernus, into whose depths flowed the river Lethe, to drink of whose waters brought forgetfulness to unhappy souls, was succeeded by the cloven-hoofed, fork-tailed Satan, god of the burning brimstone pit, into which Jehovah consigns lost souls. The graceful nymphs of the fountains and streams, the mountains and groves, passed away, and the widows of a dead deity, in funeral garb, haunt the earth.

Truly, it were better had we kept some of the fairest of the gods, rather than those that we have.

It were better to adore Apollo, with his harp strung with golden chords, than Jehovah, with his nostrils besmeared with the fumes of burning blood; better the silence of the dark waters of the Lethe than the shrieks from the red flames of Hell; better the voluptuous Venus, with her form divine, than a sexless saint with a passionless stare.

For my part, I would rather adore Ceres, goddess of the seedtime and harvest, than any of the Christian myths. I would rather join the happy husbandmen, in the ancient feasts of Ambarvalia, when the golden corn was ripe, and sings songs of praise to Ceres, than confess my sins to an immaculate priest, or crawl like a wriggling worm to a mourner's bench.

I would rather join with Virgil, the pagan poet, than with the saints in their dismal doxologies:

> "Let every swain adore her power divine,
> And milk and honey mix with sparkling wine;
> Let all the choir of clowns attend this show,
> In long procession, shouting as they go;
> Invoking her to bless their yearly stores,
> Inviting plenty to their crowded floors.
> Thus in the spring, and thus in summer's heat,
> Before the sickles touch the rip'ning wheat,
> On Ceres call; and let the lab'ring hind
> With oaken wreaths his hollow temples bind;
> On Ceres let him call, and Ceres praise,
> With uncouth dances, and with country lays."

I would rather, much rather, eat, drink and be merry, in a joyous, fearless way, than bow my head in fear of Hell while some reverend, muttering mummeries, gave me, for food and drink, a sacrificed deity's flesh and blood. I would rather dance with a sweetheart of my youth at Ceres' pagan feast, than get down on my knees at a Christian prayer-meeting.

If there are any all-observing gods they must be filled with pity at the sight of Christian worship. That is, if they are honest and healthy.

I love the Muses of Mythology, just as I loathe the saints of Christianity. Calliope, the Muse of epic poetry, with the trumpet in her hand; Clio, the Muse of history, holding the half-opened scroll; Melpomene, the Muse of tragedy, holding the tragic mask; Euterpe, the Muse of music, with her two celestial flutes; Erato, the Muse of love, playing on her nine-stringed golden lyre; Terpsichore, the Muse of dance and song, of gayety and grace, that distinguishes human beings from preachers; Urania, the Muse of astronomy, holding a globe, and tracing the figures of the science of mathematics with a wand—she knew that the earth is round, even though the inspired Scriptures declare it flat; Thalia, the Muse of comedy, with the comic mask and the crooked staff; Polyhymnia, the Muse of eloquence, with her fore-finger upon her lips.

The world might well worship these nine Muses, these divine daughters of Mnemosyne, but it has no use whatever for a cloistered monk.

The world could truly love Pomona, goddess of the fruits, and Flora, goddess of the flowers, and Pales, goddess of the flocks and fields; but it takes a strong stomach to endure a god of Hell-and-damnation.

Cerberus, the demon with three canine heads, with his body covered with snakes, who kept the gate of Pluto's palace, and Chimaera, with a head of a devouring lion, the body of a goat and the tail of a dragon, who, like Jehovah, as described in Psalms XVIII, verse 8, vomited fire from his mouth, and the Furies, with twining serpents instead of hair growing on their hideous heads—such deities as these have been metamorphosed into the Christian gods and devils; but the fair gods of the poets, the gods and goddesses of Music and Love, of the Arts and Sciences, of the Seedtime and Harvest, of the Flocks and Fields, of the Bread and Wine, of the Feast and Dance—these divinities that inspired Greek art and Greek philosophy, these divinities of Life and Passion, lie crushed beneath the heels of the joy-hating Jehovah and his black-robed priests.

The fair gods fled when Hypatia, the last of the Greek philosophers, was flayed alive by insane Christians; and the sacred tripods, torn from the demolished temple of Apollo at Delphi, adorned the Hippodrome of the bloody Constantine, the founder of the Christian creed; and all we have are the vindictive Father, the sacrificed Son, the melancholy Holy Ghost, and Satan, the Lord of Hell.

1. The War that was Fought in Heaven

It seems strange that the inspired Scriptures do not contain a history of the war that, we are told, was once fought to a finish in Heaven, between Jehovah and Satan; for upon the result of that conflict rests the entire structure of orthodox theology. The saint that saw things on the Island of Patmos makes mere mention of it in his "Book of Revelations." Perhaps a more detailed account of this war was told in the lost "Book of the Wars of the Lord," spoken of in the twenty-first chapter of Numbers, verse fourteen. Be this as it may, it is to the poet Milton that the Christian world is indebted for an elaborate revelation of the Great War in Heaven gathered from ancient legends and mythologies, that tell of the cause, the beginning and conclusion of the battles that ages ago took place on the golden streets, when Jehovah, commanding in his army two-thirds of the angels, finally routed the hosts of Satan, who only had one-third of the angels on his side.

Satan was defeated by overpowering numbers. If he had had the odds, he would doubtless have whipped Jehovah, and would be sitting on the throne of Heaven today, with Jehovah occupying Hell. There can be little doubt of this, as ancient tradition declares that the war was fought to settle the dispute as to who should sit upon the throne, Jehovah or Satan, and reign King of Heaven.

The War of Heaven was not like the bloody wars of Earth. As Jehovah and Satan, as well as all the angelic soldiers, were immortals, none were killed. They were badly beaten up, but all escaped with their lives. Jehovah's victory consisted in slowly, but surely, by the strength of his superior numbers, pushing the hosts of Satan to the walls of Heaven, and tumbling them all headlong into Hell.

What a sight it would have been to mortal eyes to have beheld Satan and his legions wildly plunging through the elements to the flaming pit! The distance, we are told, was so great that it took nine days for them to reach there. Milton graphically describes the nine-days' plunge:

> "Hell heard the insufferable noise; Hell saw Heaven, ruining from Heaven, and would have fled Affrighted; but strict Fate had cast too deep Her dark foundations, and too fast had bound. Nine days they fell; confounded Chaos roared, And felt tenfold confusion in their fall.
> Through his wild anarchy; so huge a rout
> Encumbered him with ruin. Hell at last,
> Yawning, received them whole, and on them closed."

Shocked and stunned, battered and bruised, Satan still had some fight in him. Legend says that his left leg was broken in the fall, and that he has limped ever since, but even that did not subdue his proud spirit. He mounted the throne of Hell and called around him his most valiant angels.

No matter where kings and gods abide, whether in Heaven, Hell or Earth, thrones are provided for them. This is part of our religious and social system.

Milton thus describes Satan mounting the throne of Hell as soon as he could pull himself together after his fearful fall:

> "High on a throne of royal state, which far
> Outshone the wealth of Ormus and of Ind,
> Or where the gorgeous East, with richest hand, Showers on her kings barbaric pearl and gold, Satan exalted sat, by merit raised
> To that bad eminence; and, from despair

> Thus high uplifted beyond hope, aspires
> Beyond thus high; insatiate to pursue
> Vain war with Heaven."

Of the deliberations of that first court in Hell, the introduction to Book II, *Paradise Lost*, says: "The consultation begun, Satan debates whether another battle is to be hazarded for the recovery of Heaven. Some advise it, others dissuade."

Say what you will of them, Satan and some of his angels had the grit in them, to talk about tackling Jehovah again, entrenched as he was behind the bulwarks of Heaven with superior fighting forces.

Finally, after many arguments pro and con as to the probable outcome of an attempt to scale the walls of Heaven and engage once more in battle Jehovah and his hosts, Baron von Beelzebub, who ranks next to the royal Satan himself, arose and thus spoke :

> "What if we find
> Some easier enterprise? There is a place—
> If ancient and prophetic fame in Heaven
> Err not,—another world, the happy seat
> Of some new race, called Man, about this time
> To be created, like to us, though less
> In power and excellence.
>   *   *   *
> Thither let us bend our thoughts, to learn
> What creatures there inhabit, of what mould
> Or substance, how endued, and what their power,
> And where their weakness—how attempted best,
> By force or subtlety. Though Heaven be shut,
> And Heaven's high Arbitrator sit secure
> In his own strength, this place may lie exposed."

The War that was Fought in Heaven

The proposition looked good to Satan. He immediately made up his mind to break his way out of Hell, alone by himself, and reconnoiter the new world, providing it was already in existence. If it proved to be of any vantage ground, he proposed to "benevolently assimilate it." Therefore he

> "Puts on swift wings, and towards the gates of Hell Explores his solitary flight."

It was a terrible trip. Plunging downwards into Hell was one thing, but climbing out was another. The poet biographer vividly pictures it:

> "Sometimes
> He scours the right-hand coast, sometimes the left;
> Now shaves with level wing the deep, then soars
> Up to the very concave towering high."

Jehovah had done a great piece of work when he built Hell. Or, maybe Hell and Heaven were never built—maybe they always were. There is no account to be found in Holy Writ, that I know of, that tells of their construction. That they actually exist, however, is proven by all theological authorities.

To proceed with the poet's description of Satan's trip out of Hell:

> "At last appear
> Hell-bounds, high reaching to the horrid roof,
> And thrice threefold the gates.
> Threefolds were brass,
> Three iron, three of adamantine rock
> Impenetrable, impaled with circling fire,
> Yet unconsumed."

The War that was Fought in Heaven

These gigantic gates of Hell were open when Satan and his defeated army of angels came tumbling in; they were closed and locked now.

It was a cute piece of strategy on the part of Jehovah.

However, like many an earthly army general, Jehovah appears to have blundered after he had locked the place up. Somebody had to be entrusted with the key to the gates. It was entirely too big and clumsy an article for Jehovah to carry about his person, neither did he want to have it lying around loose in Heaven. So he hunted up the ugliest female angel he could find in his kingdom, placed her in Hell with the key, and had her lock the gates from the inside. She was the worst looking fright that the inspired saints have ever told about. She

> "Seemed woman to the waist, and fair;
> But ended foul in many a scaly fold
> Voluminous and vast, a serpent armed
> With mortal sting.
> About her middle round
> A cry of hell-hounds never-ceasing barked,
> With wide Cerberian mouths, full loud, and rung
> A hideous peal.
> Yet when they list, would creep,
> If ought disturbed their noise, into her womb,
> And kennel there; yet there still barked and howled
> Within unseen."

She was, we are told,

> "The snaky sorceress that sat
> Fast by Hell-gate, and kept the fatal key."

The War that was Fought in Heaven

Jehovah should have felt fairly secure with Hell in her charge. Perhaps he thought that the bare sight of her might throw even Satan into spasms. But, in order to make it still more difficult for Satan to make his escape, Jehovah also placed at the gates of Hell a monster goblin.

> "Black it stood as Night,
> Fierce as ten Furies, terrible as Hell,
> And shook a dreadful dart."

But neither the goblin, nor the frightful sorceress with the barking hell-hounds, could terrify Satan. He sized up the goblin and defied him:

> "Whence, and what art thou, execrable shape!
> That darest, though grim and terrible, advance
> Thy miscreated front athwart my way
> To yonder gates?
> Through them I mean to pass,
> That be assured, without leave asked of thee.
> Retire, or taste thy folly, and learn by proof,
> Hell-born, not to contend with spirits of Heaven!"

And then the two, Satan and the goblin, squared themselves for the fight. And then the "snaky sorceress that sat fast by Hell-gate, and kept the fatal key," "with hideous outcry rushed between" and spoke:

> "O father! what intends thy hand," she cried, "Against thy only son! What fury, O son!
> Possesses thee to bend that mortal dart
> Against thy father's head!"

The War that was Fought in Heaven

With this Jehovah's appointed gate-keeper to Hell revealed to the two combatants a scandal, the like of which cannot be found outside of sacred literature. Milton records the tale in Book II, Paradise Lost. It runs as follows:

> Once, long ago, in fact, so long ago that Satan himself had well nigh forgotten it, it seems that a most remarkable occurrence had taken place in Heaven. It was at a time when Satan and his angels were assembled together, conspiring against Jehovah.

The feud between Jehovah and Satan appears to have dated far into the antiquity of the two god families.

Satan was discussing with his leading angels the plans for the conquest of Heaven, when he was overtaken with an agonizing pain in his head. He almost swooned; when, all of a sudden, his forehead burst open, and the most beautiful goddess he had ever beheld stepped forth.

Now Satan had always been an ardent admirer of the fair sex; he was far more gallant by nature than Jehovah; and no sooner had his eyes rested upon the lovely vision that had just sprung from his brow, than all thoughts of his headache left him, and even, for the moment, did he forget his dreams of conquest. The fact that he was, although in a most peculiar manner, the father of the angelic maid, had no apparent effect upon Satan's sudden ardor. And so it was that he and the new-born goddess were, ere long, spooning by the jeweled banks of Jordan, dining on delicate ambrosia sandwiches, and sipping celestial nectar highballs. The result was that in due time the beautiful goddess gave birth to a Satanic offspring; and oh! horrors—what was it but the hideous goblin that had met Satan at the gates of Hell! Not only this, but the goblin itself had raped its own mother, and had thereby sired the hell-hounds that howled continuously "about her middle round"; and, to put the finishing touches to the affair, Jehovah had bewitched the once beautiful goddess, sprung from the head of his competitor, into the hideous creature that held the key to Hell.

Was ever such a scandalous mix-up as this?

Among all the gods there is only one instance approaching it, and that is when Minerva sprang full armed from the head of Jove.

But no such awful doom fell upon the pagan goddess of wisdom.

Minerva, fortunately, never fell into the hands of Jehovah of the Jews.

In magic, in deeds of the black art, both Jehovah and Satan far outclass all the other gods, heathen or Christian. Heaven and Hell, as well as the brains of the orthodox clergy, abound with the freaks of their enchantments. Ezekiel saw animals from Heaven with "four faces like human beings, and with four wings like birds, and feet like a young cow." The inspired author of Revelations saw menageries of all sorts of bewitched beasts, in both Heaven and Hell. Jehovah turned the King of Babylon into a bull, and Satan turned himself into a snake. Both have made madmen of millions of humans. It is a stand-off as to which is the best—or worst—sorcerer.

But to return to Satan and his escape from Hell. As soon as he understood the situation, and realized that it was his daughter, and his son by his daughter, and barking hounds by his son and his daughter, that blocked his passage, the paternal instinct overcame all else in his being. The frightful appearance of the outfit became overshadowed in the presence of blood relationship. He was their papa, in the bosom of his family. He was ready to challenge the whole host of Heaven for every last brat he had begotten, no matter how outrageously Jehovah had deformed them.

Whatever else may be charged up to him, Satan exhibited honor enough to stand by his own.

No priests and politicians could crucify a son of his without his putting up a fight. Satan wasn't that kind of a god.

We are told, that no sooner had the bewitched wretch that held the keys to the gates of Hell concluded her story, than Satan thus spoke:

The War that was Fought in Heaven

"Dear daughter, since thou claim'st me for thy sire,

And my fair son here show'st me the dear pledge

Of dalliance had with thee in Heaven, and joys

Then sweet, now sad to mention, through dire change

Befallen us, unforeseen, unthought of; know,

I come no enemy, but to set free

From out this dark and dismal house of pain

Both him and thee, and all the heavenly hosts

Of spirits, that, in our just pretences armed,

Fell with us from on high."

In reply to which the daughter said:

"The key of this infernal pit, by due

And by command of Heaven's all-powerful King,

I keep, by him forbidden to unlock

These adamantine gates;

* * *

But what owe I to his commands above,

Who hates me, and hath hither thrust me down

Into this gloom of Tartarus profound,

To sit in hateful office here confined,

Inhabitant of Heaven, and heavenly-born,

Here, in perpetual agony and pain,

With terrors and with clamours compassed round

Of mine own brood, that on my bowels feed?"

She was a chip of the old block. Bewitch and deform her as he would, Jehovah was unable to knock the spunk out of her. Horrible though the surroundings, she showed the same spirit that the poet puts in the mouth of her sire:

"Better to reign in Hell than serve in Heaven."

Then, with defiance upon the still fair face of the goddess, even though her body was the scaly fold of a snake, Satan's daughter took the key from her side, and

> "Towards the gate rolling her bestial train,
> Forthwith the huge portcullis high updrew,
> Which but herself, not all the Stygian powers
> Could once have moved; then in the key-hole turns
> The intricate wards, and every bolt and bar
> Of massy iron or solid rock with ease
> Unfastens: on a sudden open fly,
> With impetuous recoil and jarring sound,
> The infernal doors, and on their hinges grate
> Harsh thunder, that the lowest bottom shook
> Of Erebus.   She opened, but to shut
> Excelled her power; the gates wide open stood."

And they have been wide open ever since. Jehovah worked a spell on the hinges that put them entirely out of commission. He probably figured that it might be necessary to damn the human race in a short time, providing that Satan succeeded in making his escape, and that crowds of lost souls would be pouring into Hell so fast that no gate-keeper would be able to lock and unlock the gates to receive them.

But Satan did not wait to see whether the gates remained open, or closed again. He bade his family a hasty farewell, and flew like a streak of lightning into the elements.

At last he spied

The War that was Fought in Heaven

> "Far-off the empyreal Heaven,
>
> * * *
>
> once his native seat;
> And, fast by, hanging on a golden chain,
> This pendant world, in bigness as a star
> Of smallest magnitude, close by the moon."

Jehovah had just finished his six days' work of creating the earth and all it contains out of nothing, and had returned, tired out, to Heaven. There he was comfortably resting on his throne, with the gold chain that held the earth in its proper place tied around one of the legs, when all at once his fiery eyes beheld a sight that made him sit up and take notice. We are told, in the introduction to Book III, Paradise Lost, that Jehovah, "sitting on his throne, sees Satan flying towards this world, then newly created." Then spoke the victorious King of Heaven, to Christ, who was by his side:

> "Seest thou what rage
> Transports our adversary? whom no bounds
> Prescribed, no bars of Hell, nor all the chains
> Heaped on him there, nor yet the main abyss
> Wide interrupt, can hold; so bent he seems
> On desperate revenge, that shall redound
> Upon his own rebellious head. And now,
> Through all restraint broke loose, he wings his way
> Not far off Heaven, in the precincts of light,
> Directly towards the new created world."

Every Sunday School scholar, with budding brain filled with the mysteries of theology, knows what shortly happened; how Satan, transforming himself into a handsome serpent, seduced Eve, and thereby brought upon the human race Jehovah's wrath and curse;

how, for centuries, doctors of divinity have been busy baptizing and saving a few of us, while Jehovah has been still busier dooming and damning the most of us; how the sacrifices and salvation of Jehovah have been pitted against the sorceries of Satan.

To the strictly neutral, viewing this age-long celestial feud, it is hard to determine which of the two deities is the most vindictive and vicious—the one that, with the assurance that she would become as one of the gods, tempted the woman to disobey a command that was cunningly set like a trap to catch her, or the one that, in his all-fired wrath at being buncoed by Satan, doomed and damned the woman and her posterity. If Satan had inspired a book, as Jehovah is reputed to have done, he might have told an entirely different story than the doctors of divinity have endorsed. Anyway, it seems unfair to judge the conquered by the testimony of his victorious foe. The sorceries and scandals of Satan, that, it is charged, have filled the Christian world with terror, bear only the one-sided testimony of Jehovah's friend; perhaps a candid investigation by a neutral will place Satan in a different light.

2. Satan Wanders the Earth

Ask the average Christian, "Where does Satan abide?" and most likely his answer will be, "in Hell." Yet the evidence is that Satan has no use whatever for Hell, that he makes the earth his home, and that, if he were able, he would rescue all his heaven-born angels, and earth-born lost soul, from the brimstone pit, and move them, bag and baggage, together with himself, to Heaven. The inspired Scriptures clearly disclose that Jehovah is powerful enough to hold every creature in Hell that he has a grudge against, except Satan. Him he cannot handle. In the Book of Job we learn that Satan spends his time "going to and fro in the earth, and walking up and down in it," and so late a Scriptural authority as St. Peter declares that Satan, "as a roaring lion, walketh about, seeking whom he may devour."

Satan was evidently living in or about Jerusalem at the time Jesus was there, for, we are told, he picked up Jesus one day and flew to the pinnacle of the temple with him, from whence the entire world, which was then flat, was visible to the naked eye, and offered him its rulership if he would renounce Jehovah and ally himself to Satan. From ancient legends, that bear the same evidence of veracity as the story of the virgin birth of Christ, we learn that Satan took up his residence on the earth some time previous to his breaking up Adam's happy home in Eden. It appears that Adam was married before Eve made her appearance, and that his first wife's name was Lilith. Where the lady came from is not recorded. Maybe she was an angel dropped from Heaven. Or, perhaps, Jehovah created her, as he did Eve, from one of Adam's bones. We do not know.

Howbeit, wherever she hailed from, Lilith did not get along well with Adam, and soon left him. Satan met her, was smitten with her charms, amd married her. Legend pictures her as beautiful beyond compare – a veritable vampire.

Satan may still be living with Lilith. Goethe, in his tragedy of *Faust*, makes her appear among the witches on the Brocken, on Walpurgis-Night, and thus has Satan described her:

"That's Lilith,

Adams first wife, Of her rich locks beware!

That Charm in which she's parallel'd by few;

When in its toils a youth she doth ensnare,

He will not soon escape, I promise you."

We are told that Satan also took to himself as wives three of the daughters of Eve – Naama, Igereth and Machalath. There was no race suicide in the Satan family. Lilith alone gave birth to four hundred and seventy-eight legions of children. As a legion is supposed to be composed of six thousand, Lilith became the mother of nearly two million youngsters. How many the other wives bore is not given. Probably about the same number. These children, half human and half Satanic, were called jinns.[i]

From the foregoing it will readily be seen that Satan makes this world his home. However, from a theological point of view, and which can be easily proven by blind faith, Satan may occupy both Hell and Earth at the same time.

According to the theologians, the world has been overrun with Satan's offspring, especially of the female sex, until within comparatively recent years. They were wizards and witches when assuming human form, and millions of them have been hung and burned at

---

[i] The reader will find brief mention of them, and also mention of Lilith, in the Encyclopedia Britannica.

the stake by Jehovah's priests. Their souls are in Hell. The saints that burned them at the stake are in Heaven.

What different conditions might exist in Heaven and Hell if Satan had come out victorious in his war with Jehovah! Satan might then be occupying the throne of Heaven, and Jehovah might be wandering the earth, an exile god. Jehovah's defeated army of angels might be torturing in Hell, while Satan's angels were promenading the golden boulevards. The world's scholars and scientists, gone to eternal torture for daring to investigate and reason, might have been saved, while the world's plunderers and princes, ordained, say the Scriptures, by Jehovah, that are singing hallelujahs around the heavenly throne, might be sizzling in the brimstone pit; the splendid souls, lost forever, that have filled the world with song and story, with music and the drama, might be making Heaven happy, while the saints of the Holy Inquisition, welcomed to glory, might be mingling with the bats of Inferno, that they resembled so much when on earth; the peaceful heathen, headed for red Hell, might exchange places with the warring Christians, washed in the blood of the lamb. The brains and beauty and brilliancy of earth might be occupying Heaven, and the divinely ordained war-lords and landlords and job-lords, the exploiters and extortioners, might be in Hell, if Satan had won the war he fought with Jehovah.

Of course, we can only surmise all this. It is not safe to give any creature unlimited power and authority. Perhaps Satan would have been just as vindictive as Jehovah, had he been King of Heaven. He might have demanded the same sacrifices of brutes and humans, to satisfy his awful wrath, that Jehovah has demanded. He might have even had one of his own offspring by Lilith crucified, and Christians might be washing their sins away in the blood of a jinn. Jehovah, had be been defeated and driven from Heaven by Satan, might have bred millions of witches to afflict mankind, and Satan might have inspired some saint to write the eighteenth verse of the twenty-second chapter of Exodus: "Thou shalt not suffer a witch to live." Satan, instead of being a demon, might have been a merciful god, like Jehovah, and have commanded his faithful followers to kill every male and female of the enemy, old and young, save the best looking of the maidens, and to take these for their own lust, as recorded in the thirty-first chapter of Numbers, verses 17-18. Satan might have ordained human slavery and polygamy, as Jehovah did, were he in Jehovah's place. He might be filling Hell with scholars and Heaven with lunatics, in the regular orthodox manner, if he was God Almighty.

It is hard to tell what would have happened if Satan had won the crown.

It does not seem, though, that he could possibly have made things much worse than have Jehovah and his ordained powers that be. All of Satan's witches combined never caused anywhere near the desolation that a single one of Jehovah's warlords have. Besides, we must remember, it is Satan that inspired the world's scholars and thinkers, and its rebels against oppression. Jehovah does not believe in science, nor in human liberty. Jehovah has ordained every doctor of delusion that ever occupied a pulpit, every tyrant that ever sat on a throne. None of these have been Satan's followers.

True, Satan is charged with some cruel deeds, but most of his sorceries are in the nature of scandals. In the jocular sense of the word, he is a regular "devil." Satan loves a joke. This can hardly be said of Jehovah. Take, for instance, the story of St. Anthony, the founder of Christian monasticism—the first of the order of holy hoboes, known as monks. Everything in this world was wicked, and under the control of Satan, in St. Anthony's eyes, and the wickedest of all was woman. Satan had ruined her, Jehovah had cursed her, and, according to Christian theology, she alone was the cause of all our ills. Moreover, it was believed and taught that a large portion of the women were witches, the daughters of Satan.

From his early youth St. Anthony was filled with piety. He renounced the pleasures of this world and made himself miserable with thoughts of God. To eat a square meal was a sin, and a woman's smile savored of perdition itself. In order to thoroughly sanctify himself he left his home and wandered in the wilderness, penniless, shelterless, and nearly naked, subsisting on herbs and stagnant water. Satan was on his trail, and, assuming the form of a beautiful maiden, did his best to make St. Anthony fall. But it was of no use. St. Anthony had so thoroughly and religiously mortified his body that he had become temptation proof.

From that time on, Satan, in some female form, has oft times been a terror to Jehovah's celibates. He has tantalized many a holy father till he well nigh went crazy. Some of the weaker ones have emasculated themselves in order to make sure of saving their souls. They literally followed the inspired injunction, and "made themselves eunuchs for the Kingdom of Heaven's sake." Origen was one of this number. Others, alas! have scandalized their holy calling, and have fallen victims to the charms of Satan's wicked women.

One of the meanest tricks that Satan has played, in order to besmirch the good name of some of Jehovah's saints that were proof against his cunning wiles, was to impersonate the saint himself. "Occasionally," says W.E.H. Lecky, in his *History of the Rise and Influence of Rationalism in Europe* (1866), "with a still more refined malice, the Evil One assumed the appearance of some noted divine, in order to bring discredit upon his character; and an astonished maiden saw, prostrate at her feet, the form of one she knew to be a bishop, and whom she believed to be a saint!"

It wasn't the saintly bishop at all that had entered the maiden's boudoir and, like a love-sick swain, had prostrated himself at her feet; it was Satan, the scamp, in the livery of Heaven, besmirching the immaculate character of the man of God. We know this to be a fact, because the scandalized bishop, and all his clergy, said so; and all the faithful believed it.

I think sometimes the maiden might have had her doubts.

Exposures of this kind, however, only occurred when the simple-hearted maiden, in order to protect herself, screamed for help, and Satan, in the form of a priest, took to his heels; or when, as often happened, an unsuspecting husband (or, perhaps, sometimes he was suspicious), returned unexpectedly to his home and found his wife in a compromising situation with a holy father. Such cases were frequently taken to court. But it was always proven, by clerical witnesses, that the priest in question was in his own virtuous chamber at the time of the scandal, piously saying his prayers; and the judge so rendered his decision, and pronounced Satan the guilty culprit.

Satan's magic power of impersonation was so great that women were known to give birth to children that were the perfect image of the parish priest. A neighborhood scandal of this sort, that naturally, in spite of his innocence, caused considerable embarrassment to the priest, was one of Satan's special delights. It not only embarrassed the holy father, but it also irritated Jehovah sitting on his throne.

Public exposures, however, did not always accompany Satan's amorous adventures among the fair sex. Ofttimes, alas! the fair damsel, or buxom dame of some tired toiler of the soil, or, perchance, the blooming bride of some aristocratic but antiquated lord, mistaking Satan for her father confessor, slipped and fell. Nor did Satan, strange to say, desert such an affinity when he found that she had no inclination whatever to spurn his advances, and thus bring shame and reproach upon the innocent, pious priest he was impersonating.

At other times, as admitted, Satan perpetrated acts of cruelty as enormous, almost, as those charged to Jehovah. A notable instance is the way, with Jehovah's assistance, he outraged Job. It seems that at this time Jehovah and Satan were on quite familiar terms again, for, we are told in the first chapter of the Book of Job, verses 6 and 7: Now there was a day when the sons of God came to present themselves before the Lord, and Satan came also among them. And the Lord said unto Satan, Whence comest thou? Then Satan answered the Lord, and said, From going to and fro in the earth, and from walking up and down in it."

A conversation concerning earthly matters then took place between the two majesties, in which the saintly character of Jehovah's friend Job, a large cattle and slave owner, was enlarged upon. Jehovah claimed that no power in Heaven or Hell could make a rebel of Job. Satan boasted that if Jehovah would turn Job over to him for a few days, he would make him curse his god to his face. Jehovah called the bluff, and told Satan he could do anything to Job but kill him. So Satan flew back to earth and went after Job without mercy. He had all his cattle and slaves killed, and also all his sons and daughters.

If he had saved some of the young girls for the soldiers that did the slaughtering, Satan's massacre of the Job family would have equaled Jehovah's massacre of the Midianites.

But the question arises, Who was the guiltiest in this slaughter, Satan or Jehovah? According to the divinely inspired account, Satan had no power over Job, or at least would not assume any power, until Jehovah granted it, which is vouched for in the first chapter of Job, verse 12. It is perfectly evident that Jehovah could have stopped the slaughter if he wanted to, and it is just as evident that he let it take place in order to see what effect it would have on Job. Any honest jury would make Jehovah *particeps criminis* in the case, and any honest judge would sentence the two alike.

Another massacre, that is charged to Satan's account by the theologians, is recorded in the second chapter of St. Matthew, verse 16, which reads: "Then Herod, when he saw that he was mocked of the wise men, was exceeding wroth, and sent forth, and slew all the children that were in Bethlehem, and in all the coasts thereof, from two years old and under."

The theologians charge that this was Satan's work, in an attempt to kill the infant Christ, the son of Jehovah, who, as told in Milton's *Paradise Lost*, had eternally existed in Heaven, as a full grown god, before he became an earthly infant. Heretical students of history claim that this massacre never took place—that it was never heard of until years after the time alluded to, when Christian priests wrote it into the New Testament in an attempt to make it fulfill an alleged prophecy of Jeremiah. With this doubt as to the slaughtering of the Bethlehem infants, Jehovah, with his record of the slaughtering of all the first-born of Egypt in a night, still holds the championship as a baby butcher.

Outside of his killing off Job's family—which, as noted, appears to have been a partnership arrangement between himself and Jehovah—Satan is quite guiltless of manslaughter. He is much more of a mischief-maker than a murderer. He never built machines to torture heretics. He never burned them at the stake. He does not lead armies of Christians into bloody war. It is always the God Jehovah that the war-lords pray to for help in battle. They never were known to pray to Satan. The plundering powers that be are all ordained by Jehovah. They are his own. St. Paul says so. Satan may tempt a hungry man to steal a loaf of bread, but he is not responsible for the social system that drove the man to hunger. Jehovah's ordained powers that be attended to this. Satan may tempt a girl to sell her body, but he doesn't pay the starvation wage that filled her soul with despair. The owner of her job is a child of the God Jehovah, a liberal contributor to religious work, a pillar in the church. Such sins as attending theatres, dancing and card-playing may be charged to Satan, but child-slavery is a Christian institution. Satan may build the breweries, but it's Jehovah's faithful that operate the ammunition factories. Satan may pull off a prize fight, but it's Jehovah and his ordained rulers that turn the world into a human slaughter-house.

3. Some of Satan's Sinners and Jehovah's Saints

Census taking, like the pursuit of knowledge, is a sin in the sight of the God Jehovah. He forbids his followers from numbering their population. He evidently does not want the masses to know their strength.

As Jehovah is the god of the master class, and not of slaves, some light may be thrown upon what appears to be a peculiar decree, when we take into consideration that the slave-owning aristocracy of ancient Greece promulgated the same law against the slaves ascertaining their numbers. For this reason all slaves were compelled to wear different patterns of clothing, so that, meeting in public places, they could not recognize the social standing of each other. On the streets and in the market places a slave could not be told from a freeman. If they had dressed in the same sort of apparel, like the *sansculottes* of France, before the Revolution, they might have noted their overwhelming superiority of numbers over their masters, and revolted.

But, however this may be, Jehovah outlawed census taking, and Satan, discovering such to be the case, once played the mischief with Jehovah's chosen people. We read in the twenty-first chapter of the divinely inspired First Book of Chronicles: "And Satan stood up against Israel, and provoked David (that is, he dared him) to number Israel. And David said to Joab and to the rulers of the people, Go, number Israel from Beersheba even to Dan; and bring the number of them to me, that I may know it."

David doubtless knew that it would make Jehovah angry, but he wouldn't take Satan's dare.

And so the deed was done. A census was taken of the Jews, contrary to their god's decree. And their god, sitting on his throne in Heaven, flew into a rage. He clawed the air with his horned fists and blew sparks from his nostrils. Satan himself had no idea that the thing was going to drive him to such fury as it did. With his magic, so we are told, Jehovah sent a deadly pestilence upon the Jews and killed seventy-thousand of them. He probably used poisoned gas, the same as his ordained war lords use to-day. With this victorious starter to spur himself and his heavenly hosts to further deeds of valor, Jehovah started for Jerusalem. He proposed to annihilate the capital city of Israel. King David, who was scanning the skies for any approaching flying troops, much as the inhabitants of a town to-day, in time of war, scan the skies for an airship, caught sight of one of Jehovah's biggest and fiercest angels, armed with a sword, that was probably several miles long, swooping down towards the city with blood in his eye. David and his elders, as was customary with the holy men in those days, when endeavoring to soothe their god, had covered their otherwise naked bodies in sackcloth. They had doubtless, as was also the religious custom, greased their skins and rolled themselves in ashes.

At the sight of the oncoming avenging angel they fell flat upon their faces. Such humility is pleasing to Jehovah. In this respect he is much like the kings of Europe, or one of our federal judges. Jehovah saw the prostrate forms of David and his elders, saw the sackcloth and ashes scratching their hides raw, and began to cool off a bit. It flattered his vanity. So he had the advancing angel, armed with the big sword, interview one of David's soothsayers, by the name of Gad, to whom he offered terms of peace, upon condition that David immediately build a stone altar, and sacrifice thereon a number of goats and sheep so that Jehovah could smell their burning blood.

Jehovah graciously accepted the offering, and confirmed the treaty of peace, by sending from Heaven a streak of fire that consumed the slaughtered animals piled on the altar. All of which is recorded in the chapter of the First Book of Chronicles already referred to.

An entirely different account of this census taking, and the fury of Jehovah that followed, is found, strange to relate, in the twenty-fourth chapter of the Second Book of Samuel. Here we are informed that it was Jehovah himself, and not Satan, that tempted King David to take the census.

"Great is the mystery of godliness," says the Scriptures.

This is clearly disclosed by the way the inspired writers contradict each other. It is probably done to try the faith of believers.

It is claimed, by the priests of the fourth century, that compiled the New Testament, that Jehovah's son, who was divinely doomed to be offered up in sacrifice to appease his father's wrath, was able to turn water into wine. Satan, we are told, can outclass this—he can miraculously create wine without any water. All he needs is a bunghole. Moreover, he can make any brand of wine the thirst calls for. Goethe exploits this magic power of Satan in his tragedy of *Faust*. He tells of a jolly company gathered together at a public house, with Satan present. Satan criticized the quality of wine being served, and remarked, "I am afraid the landlord to offend; Else freely would I treat each guest From my own cellar to the very best."

Then spoke one of the company, "Out with it, then! Your doings I'll defend."

And another cried, "Give him a good glass, and straight we'll praise you one and all.

Only let not your samples be too small."

"Fetch me a gimlet," said Satan. The gimlet was brought to him, taken from the landlord's tool-basket; whereupon Satan proceeded to bore a hole in the edge of the table opposite to where one of the company was sitting. "Get me some wax, and make some stoppers," continued Satan, as he rapidly bored holes in the table in front of each guest. The wax was procured and the stoppers made, and the holes corked. Then Satan, making mystic signs, said:

> "Grapes the vine-stock bears,
> Horns the buck-goat wears!
> Wine is sap, the vine is wood,
> The wooden board yields wine as good!
> With deeper glance and true,
> The mysteries of nature view!
> Have faith, and here's a miracle!
> Your stoppers draw, and drink your fill!"

And sure enough, from every hole in the wooden table poured forth an incessant, sparkling stream of the rarest wine, of each particular brand called for, that ever tickled the palate of mortal. They all drank their fill. They became musical, and arose to their feet and sang:

> "Oh, beauteous spring, which flows so fair!"
> To which Satan warningly replied:
> "Spill not a single drop, of this beware!"

But the warning was unheeded. They were all having too glorious a time with miraculously made Sherry and Burgundy, Moselle and Madeira, Rhine wine and Champagne, flowing freely into their goblets, as fast as they emptied them, from a hole in the table. At length one of the number, singing, "Happy as cannibals are we, Or as five hundred swine," carelessly tipped his glass and spilt a portion of his wine. It immediately turned to flame; whereupon the startled bibber suddenly changed his tune, and lustily yelled.

"Help! fire! help!   Hell is burning!"

At which Satan addressed the flame, saying, "Stop, Kind element, be still, I say."

The flame obeyed its master's voice, and went out, just as the raging sea calmed down when the son of Jehovah told it to.

But alas! one of the bibulous company pulled the plug and attempted to drink from the bunghole; and the exhilarating beverage poured forth faster than he could swallow it, and ran down his whiskers and soaked into his shirt; and horrors! it was no longer wine, but flames of fire, so that the sufferer cried out aloud, "I burn! I burn!" Thereupon, we are informed, the company all drew their knives and attacked Satan.

If it had been Jehovah, instead of Satan, no doubt but that all of them would have been smitten with some deadly plague, or, like the sinners' of Sodom, suffocated with boiling brimstone. But Satan, as before remarked, is not that kind of a merciful and loving god. He didn't want to kill them, he was just having fun with them. So he made some more mystic signs—something as the preachers do when they shut their eyes, hold their two hands tight together, and twist their necks downward when talking to Jehovah—and spoke these words:

> "Visionary scenes appear!
> Words delusive cheat the ear!
> Be ye there, and be ye here!"

And presto! it all happened. It was just as easy as Jehovah's trick of having his priests turn bread and wine into the actual flesh and blood of a sacrificed deity.

"Where am I?" exclaimed an enchanted bacchanalian.

"What a beauteous land!"

"Vineyards! unless my sight deceives!" cried another.

"And clustering grapes, too, close at hand!" "And underneath the spreading leaves,

Some of Satan's Sinners and Jehovah's Saints

What stems there be! What grapes I see!" hilariously sang another.

At this every one seized each other by the nose, and, thinking they had hold of a luscious cluster of grapes, drew their knives, and would have cut off each others' noses, had not Satan at this moment ended the enchantment by repeating:

"Delusion, from their eyes the bandage take.

Note how the Devil loves a jest to break!"

At these words the whole company came to their senses perfectly sober.

"What was it?" said one of them.

"And was that your nose?" said another. And then they looked at the banquet table, whence had flowed the miraculous wine. There was nothing doing. Everything was dry as powder. Even the holes were gone. Nothing was left but a parched, unsatisfied sensation in their throats. Their magic host had departed.

"With my own eyes, upon a cask astride, Forth through the cellar door I saw him ride," exclaimed one of the victims of Satan's enchantment.

"Would that the wine again were flowing!" sadly remarked another.

And Satan, full of more mischief to play upon mankind, went forth into the world to ensnare the sons and daughters of men.

The trials and tribulations of Jehovah's followers, in their endeavor to escape Satan's snares, as manifested in the charms of the female sex, form one of the most prominent features in church history. All women are witches—the daughters of Satan—in one way or another; and all men are bewitched by them. Love and passion are mortal sins in the sight of the God Jehovah. They are the sorceries and scandals of Satan, by which men lose their immortal souls. "Celibacy must be chosen," said Saint Tertullian, "even though the human race should perish." And again said this same saint: "Woman, you ought to go about clad in mourning and rags, your eyes filled with tears of remorse, to make us forget that you have been mankind's destruction. Woman, you are the gate to Hell." Origen, who was one of the leading lights in deciding what was to be contained in the New Testament, declared: "Matrimony is impure and unholy; a means of sensual passion." The Apostle Paul expresses his contempt for women in his inspired epistles. He admits that it was only by the strongest sort of faith that he managed to remain in their society and still steer clear of their charms. Others only escaped the charms of Satan's fair daughters by mortifying their flesh. Many, like Saint Anthony, left the abodes of men and lived in the desert. There, by fasting and self-torture, they saved their spotless souls. Some had their bodies sewed in furs and pelts, with only a hole left large enough to breathe through and receive their scanty food. In this condition they lived for years, pure and holy, under the blazing African sun. That is, their souls were "pure and holy"; their bodies, encased from their necks to their feet in hides, with no opening save at the mouth and nostrils, became so full of filth and vermin that Satan himself, to say nothing of his wicked daughters of earth, could not endure their presence. They were safe at last in the arms of the Lord. Their only thoughts were upon death and the everlasting judgment.

Some, instead of being sewed in pelts, had themselves buried up to their necks in the torrid desert sands. Nourishment was brought to them by one of the holy fathers that wore furs. In this way they lived until their tortured bodies succumbed, and their saved souls took their flight to Heaven.

In order to subdue what the heretics call the "instincts of nature," but declared by theologians to be the "temptations of the Evil One," many "made a vow not to speak a word for years; to look at none; to hop about on one leg; to eat nothing but grass."

There was a saint by the name of Thalelaus, if the record be true, sorely tempted by Satan, day after day, through the allurements and bewitcheries of Satan's daughters. Deciding that it would be a greater victory over his sinful body, and more glory to his god, to remain pure and spotless among his fellowmen, than to hike to a desert and there mortify his person until the Devil himself could not stomach him, who saved his virtuous soul by having an iron hoop welded around his body, from his waist nearly to his knees. He limped about this way for ten years, when he became such a physical wreck that Satan's sorceries were powerless to tempt him any more.

Another, Saint Simeon by name, only ate once a week, on Sunday, and laced his body so tight with ropes that he broke out all over with running sores. His religion forbidding the luxury of a bath, and also any medical aid save "Christian Science," he finally became so offensive that no one could remain near him without fainting.

Satan gave Saint Simeon up.

The holy Saint Pachonius was tempted by Satan until, we are told, he "was driven into the desert by this inward fire." One day Satan appeared to him in the form of a voluptuous Ethiopian girl. Saint Pachonius went into a delirium, and in that state believed for the moment that he had fallen to her snares. But his piety snatched him as a "brand from the burning"; he came to himself, and recognizing who it was that sought his ruin, he struck the temptress a violent blow in the face, and sure enough immediately Satan himself stood in her place.

Satan took it all in good humor, and vanished into the air.

The scandalous affair, however, so smote the conscience of the holy father that he concluded that his only chance to obtain Heaven's forgiveness would be to sacrifice his life. He therefore wandered in the desert until he found a den infested by hyenas. Saint Pachonius stripped himself to the skin—the skin that had not known water for several years, that was covered with filth and sores and vermin—and went into the den and lay down. The hyenas sniffed him all over, but refused to eat him. They knew by the smell that he was a saint, and turned away. In the presence of such a miracle as this Saint Pachonius re-consecrated himself to holiness, and finally founded a monastery in which dwelt fourteen hundred monks.

We read that at one time "there were in Egypt alone upward of a hundred thousand monks and nuns." Great numbers of women became crazed over their lost condition, and buried themselves in convents. In this state of perpetual vows of chastity Jehovah forgave them for the ruin they had brought, through Satan's temptation, upon the male sex.

The belief that Satan was busily engaged in bringing about the downfall of men through the enticements of women, that many a beautiful maiden was an actual daughter of Satan, that a man, entering matrimony, was liable to some day find himself bound to a witch of Hell, played havoc with Christian society. Bridegrooms, seized with the fear of God, abandoned their brides on their wedding night.

Some of the holiest saints got their start in this way.

The holy Alexus suddenly left his wife on the day of their nuptials, and rushed into the desert. The holy Ammo read to his betrothed some of Paul's denunciations of women and married life. The girl saw the sinfulness of becoming a wife and mother. They both renounced their love, took vows of chastity, she becoming a nun, and he a monk.

Johannes Colybita was seized with the fear of God on his wedding night. He fled into the desert. Finally he came back to his native town, sanctified and saved, and lived as a beggar to the end of his days.

In order to keep himself too weary to be wicked, too sore to succumb to Satan's sorceries, Saint Barnabas had a sharp stone inserted in his foot.

Another saint, Maccarius, cured himself of the lust of the flesh by sitting naked in a nest of red ants.

The migration of the saints to the desert finally became unpopular; they preferred remaining in worldly society, even though they thereby risked losing their souls. Europe became literally overrun with holy monks. They performed miracles equal to those of Jehovah or Satan.

One of the greatest of the European saints was Bernard. Of him Martin Luther said: "If there ever was a true and God-fearing monk, it was Saint Bernard. I have never heard or read of any equal to him, arid I esteem him higher than all the monks and priests of the world."

Some of Satan's Sinners and Jehovah's Saints

And Luther knew how hard it is to live a holy life. Satan was at his heels continually.[i]

Of the holiness of Saint Bernard there can be no doubt. Church history tells us that he "tortured his body in a most terrible manner, and together with his monks often subsisted solely on beech leaves and a kind of miserable barley bread. When, occasionally, to strengthen his system, he partook of a porridge with oil and honey, he wept bitterly over his weakness." He finally became so holy that he was able to perform all manner of miracles. We are told that at one time a marble image of Christ, portraying the crucifixion, climbed down from the cross and walked up to Saint Bernard and embraced him. At another time, after a long fast, Saint Bernard, while praying before a stone statue of the Virgin Mary, became extremely weak from hunger. The stone statue of the Holy Virgin, seeing his distress, offered its breast to the saint, and he drank from it copious draughts of the finest milk he had ever tasted. Once, in the Cathedral of Speier, he approached an image of the Holy Virgin, and said: "I salute thee, oh Queen!" The image of the Holy Virgin politely bowed its head and replied: "We thank thee, our beloved Bernard."

Saint Francis of Assisi was another remarkable example of overcoming the "world, the flesh and the Devil." He became so holy that no wicked daughter of Satan could lead him astray. He made his living by begging from door to door, and all the discarded food given him he dumped into an iron pot that he carried. When he became so hungry that he could not stand it any longer he ate from the accumulated mess. The condition of the various articles of food can be well imagined. It was like dining from a garbage can. He treated all manner of animals as brothers and sisters. One time he discovered a louse crawling on his greasy cowl. Saint Francis tenderly took it up in his fingers, kissed it and said: "Dear sister louse, praise the Lord with me." Then he placed it back in his frowzy hair, from whence it had wandered. He subdued his sinful body by frequently rolling on a bed

---

i   Later on a sketch of Luther's experiences with Satan will be given.

of thorns, wading in frozen water up to his neck, and lying naked in the snow. He also performed miracles.

Interesting biographies are told of the female saints who overcame the sorceries and scandals of Satan and became the sinless brides of Christ. Saint Theresa of Spain, at the age of seventeen, saw heavenly visions. Christ himself at length noted her holiness and appeared to her in person, and offered his hand in marriage. She married him, and became Abbess of a convent at Pastrana. There she gathered together numerous other brides of Christ, saved from Satan.

Saint Theresa exercised the strictest discipline over the nuns. They all went barefoot, and any disobedience was severely punished. They were tied to a mule's manger and made to eat oats and hay; they were whipped with switches; they were forced to sleep on thorns and in the snow; they drank from spittoons; dead mice were put in their mouths, the bread they ate was dipped in rotten eggs, their tongues were pierced with needles. All of which was pleasing to Jehovah—and doubtless disgusting to Satan.

In her youth Saint Catherine of Cardone, through the sorceries of Satan, fell in love. Realizing her sinful condition, she fled to a cavern and subsisted, like Saint Anthony, on herbs. She made herself a garment of thick grasses, interwoven with thorns. In this condition Satan was unable to do anything with her.

Saint Passidea of Siena used to lash herself with thorns until her body bled, and then rub salt, pepper and vinegar in the wounds. She slept in a bunk filled with cherry pits and dried peas, and, to further insure her salvation, wore an iron chemise that weighed sixty pounds.

There are two stories of Saint Agnes. One, and which is most generally accepted in theological circles, is that she was a Christian maid of Rome, who refused to marry the son of the Roman prefect, Sempronius. She was condemned to a brutal outrage, and then to be burned alive; but, when tied to the stake, the fagots would not burn. Thereupon an officer struck off her head.

Another version, and which was popular among the faithful of the Middle Ages, is that the prefect, upon her refusal to marry his son, had her driven through the streets naked to a brothel. She had no sooner entered the place, however, than her hair grew so profusely that it entirely covered her body like a garment. At the sight of the miracle all the inmates were converted to Jehovah's religion.

Another similar case is that of Saint Paula, whom an ardent lover, tempted by Satan, endeavored to betray. In the agony of her temptation Paula prayed to Jehovah for help, and Jehovah heard her prayer, and came to her rescue in a most peculiar way; he caused a heavy, long beard to suddenly grow on her face, reaching to her waist. The young man became frightened and fled.

Satan fled also.

Perhaps the most remarkable of the female saints, of which the Church calendar abounds, and who, like the male saints, escaped the sorceries and scandals of Satan, is Saint Rosa. The following description of her life is found in the papal bull that decrees her canonization. We are informed that she slept on knotty sticks of wood and on pieces of broken glass, and drank daily a pint of gall. Christ became so enraptured with such an exhibition of saintly maidenhood, that, one Palm Sunday, he appeared to her in the character of a stone-cutter, and offered himself in heavenly matrimony in these words: "Rosa, treasure of my life, thou shalt be my bride!" The Virgin Mary, who had accompanied Christ, thereupon congratulated Rosa, and exclaimed: "See what a great honor my son bestows on thee!" And so the marriage of Christ and Saint Rosa took place.

And after that, when Saint Rosa was reading her prayers, Christ would appear on the inscribed words, and smile upon her; when she was sewing he would come and sit in her sewing basket and talk to her. At times he would visit his other brides—all the nuns in Christendom were his brides—and then Saint Rosa would go wild with jealousy. But even then Satan could not tempt her. She remained true to the polygamous god she had married.

That she was honored beyond all other brides of Christ is shown by the treatment her mother-in-law bestowed upon her; we are informed that the Holy Virgin served her as chambermaid for twenty-one years, and never failed to arouse her for early mass in these words: "Rise, dear daughter; it is time for mass." And Saint Rosa would arise, and go to church, and eat the flesh and drink the blood of her sacrificed husband.

To tell of all the wonders performed by the holy saints would fill volumes. In strictly Catholic countries today the legends of their miracles, that are faithfully believed, are without number. Holy men rode crocodiles across the Nile; they led furious dragons with a string; they set snow afire; they made iron float and fruit grow on willow trees; they hitched Satan to a plow and made him furrow the field.

Over a real saint, Satan has no power of sorcery or scandal.

However, with some of the pretended ones, he appears at times, to have raised particular hades.

4. Satan and his Transformations

One of the most successful sorceries of Satan is what the Rev. Doctors of Delusion term "lycanthropy." The word is from the Greek, *lykanthropos*, which means a "wolf-man." The Anglo-Saxon werwulf, more commonly known as were-wolf, means the same. Lycanthropy is the magical ceremony performed by Satan that makes a human being temporarily change himself or herself into a wolf. It can also transform the victim into a cat, or other animal. It is explained by theological writers with the same logic that shows how a priest can change bread and wine into the body and blood of Christ. Such sorceries are easy with either Satan or Jehovah. Also with the heathen gods. The gods and devils of the heathen religions can perform every trick that the Christian religion boasts. They practice lycanthropy, witchcraft, produce miracles, and cause women to give birth to ghost-begotten babies. They also ordain war-chiefs and big medicine men to rule and rob the people.

But to return to Satan and his practice of lycanthropy among the Christians, which was common in Europe, and also among the New England Puritans, until recent times, and which is still going on in some of the strictly Catholic countries.

Says Lecky:

> "That the Devil could assume the form of any animal he pleased, * * * presented no difficulty to those who remembered that the first appearance of that personage on earth was as a serpent, and that on one oc-

casion a legion of devils (his offspring, born of his union with Adam's first wife, Lilith, and other women) had entered into a herd of swine."

This being a gospel fact, can any of the faithful doubt the ability of Satan to practice lycanthropy, and thus turn men and women into animals? Did not Jehovah practice the art himself when he transformed Nebuchadnezzar into a bull, and is not Satan just as powerful a god as Jehovah? In all the long centuries in which Christianity ruled by the grace of God and the Holy Inquisition, when faith was universal and education outlawed, when to doubt was to suffer torture and death, are there not countless exhibitions of Satan's unlimited power as a sorcerer, chief among which were lycanthropy and witchcraft? Even to-day to deny these divinely vouched-for sorceries, and to cease hanging and burning witches, is rank infidelity. Read the inspired word, as found in the twenty-second chapter of Exodus, verse 18:

"Thou shalt not suffer a witch to live."

"Satan's power to turn people into animals was accepted," says Lecky, "by the greatest and most orthodox theologians, by the inquisitors who were commissioned by the popes, and by the law courts of most countries." He records that "in the first half of the seventeenth century, the civil power uniformly exerted its energies for the destruction of witches. It was between the publication of the Works of Montaigne and of Charron, that Boguet was presiding at the tribunal of St. Claude, where he is said to have burnt 600 persons, chiefly for lycanthropy. A few years later fifty executions at Douay took place; and in 1642 Cardinal Mazarin wrote a letter to the Bishop of Evreux, congratulating him warmly on the successful zeal he had manifested in the subject."

What a beautiful place to live in, this world will be, if the present-day prayerful efforts of the Church and the plutocracy to restore the old-time Christian faith to power can be made successful!

Some of the pranks that Satan plays practicing his art would be amusing if they did not form part of our holy religion; other sorceries, charged to him by the clergy, become tragedies in the light of modern knowledge. Lunacy, imbecility, hypochondria and hysteria, are all sorceries of Satan. Jehovah himself, according to the Old Testament, and his divinely begotten son, according to the New, firmly believe this.

Robert G. Ingersoll, in the first lecture he ever delivered,[i] entitled "Progress," describes the religious insanity—and the Christian religion, together with the exploitation and wars carried on by the Christians, has caused more insanity than any other agency, not even excepting syphilis—that at one time overran society. He says:

> "We can account for a man suffering death for what he believes to be right. He knows that he has the sympathy of all the truly good, and he hopes that his name will be gratefully remembered in the far future, and above all, he hopes to win the approval of a just God. But the man who confessed himself guilty of being a wizard (and many did) knew that his memory would be execrated and expected that his soul would be eternally lost. * * * They considered their case hopeless, they confessed and died without a prayer. These things are enough to make one think that sometimes the world becomes insane and that the earth is a vast asylum without a keeper."

It does look that way. Nor is the insanity necessarily a witchcraft craze. It takes other forms. It will plunge itself into the bloody carnival of war because some prince or plutocrat commands it to. It will labor like a galley slave to produce vast stores of wealth and

---

[i] Pekin, Illinois, 1860

then stand meekly by while a parasite takes it away. It will scorn a philosopher and follow a fool to destruction. It will embrace lies and repudiate truth.

It ill becomes the masses of today, led by the nose by preachers, editors and politicians, to boast much superiority over their forebears that hung and burnt witches.

Ingersoll relates in his lectures some of the witchcraft cases:

> "In the time of James the First, a man was burned in Scotland for having produced a storm at sea for the purpose of drowning one of the royal family."

Of course it would be hard to find a professing Christian today who believes that anybody, charmed by Satan, could produce a storm at sea. It seems too ridiculous. Only such reasonable stories as Jesus Christ, charmed by Jehovah, walking on the sea, are now accepted.

> "A woman was tried before Sir Matthew Hale, one of the most learned and celebrated lawyers of England, for having caused children to vomit crooked pins. She was also charged with nursing demons. Of course she was found guilty, and the learned Judge charged the jury that there was no doubt as to the existence of witches, that all history, sacred and profane, and that the experience of every country proved it beyond any manner of doubt. And the woman was either hanged or burned for a crime for which it was impossible for her to be guilty."

> "People were burned for causing frosts in summer, for destroying crops with hail, for causing cows to become dry and even for souring beer. * * * At Basle, in 1474, a rooster was tried, charged with having laid an egg, and as rooster eggs were used only in making witch ointment it was a serious charge, and everyone, of course, admitted that

Satan and his Transformations

the Devil must have been the cause, as roosters could not very well lay eggs without some help."

The rooster, we are told, "was duly convicted and he, together with his miraculous egg, were publicly and with all due solemnity burned in the public square."

"A hog and six pigs were tried for having killed, and partially eaten a child; the hog was convicted and executed, but the pigs were acquitted on the ground of their extreme youth."

Satan's hogs, that devoured children, were put to death. Jehovah's hogs, that devour them in the cotton mills, are honored in Christian society.

"As late as 1740 a cow was tried on a charge of being possessed of the devil."

In those days the priests were the only teachers and wrote all the books that the people were allowed to read— that is, those who could read.

"The history of the Britons," says Ingersoll in the lecture quoted, "written by the Archdeacons of Mon-mouth and Oxford, was immensely popular. According /to their account, Brutus, a Roman, conquered England, built London, and called the country Britain after himself. During his time it rained blood for three days."

This was not Satan's doings. It was Jehovah that rained the blood. His ordained rulers still rain blood.

According to these priestly historians, "a monster came from the sea, and after having devoured a great many common people, finally swallowed the king himself. They say that King Arthur was not born like ordinary mortals, but was formed by a magical contrivance made by a wizard. That he was particularly lucky killing giants, that he killed one in France that used to eat several people every day, and that this giant was clothed with garments made entirely of the beards of kings that he had killed and eaten. * * * One of the authors of this book was promoted for having written an authentic history of his country."

He was apparently about as reliable an authority as the editors of our capitalist papers.

The existence of were-wolves—human beings that Satan transformed into wolves—was religiously vouched for as late as the early part of the eighteenth century. Those that believed in Satan's were-wolves were about as sensible as those that believe in Jehovah's war-wolves. Scholars declare that the were-wolves were raving maniacs. It is likely that the war-wolves, some day, will be classed in the same category.

An English writer, Frank Hamel, in a work called "Human Animals," gives, among other myths and superstitions, an interesting account of these were-wolves. The courts were as busy trying were-wolves as they are now trying bootleggers in prohibition territory. Men and women were tried in court and convicted, oft times by their own confession. A man by the name of Giles Garnier was tried and convicted and burned alive in France in 1573 on the charge "of devouring children while in the form of a wolf. He pleaded guilty, declaring that he changed his shape by rubbing an ointment prepared by Satan on his body. He would have been an easy convert at a revival meeting were he living now.

In 1598, at Angers, Jacques Roblet was found guilty and condemned to death for having as a were-wolf, ate "women, lawyers and bailiffs, though the last named he found tough and tasteless."

During the last years of the sixteenth century Satan started a regular epidemic of lycanthropy in France. In 1598 a tailor was torn to pieces by a mob in Paris on the testimony of devout Christians who swore they had seen him prowling at night in the form of a wolf.

People who believe that Satan flew with Christ in his arms to the pinnacle of the temple will scout this story.

We are told that Chinese peasants still believe that wolves and foxes attain to 800 years of age, and that, when they are past 500, they have the power to change themselves into beasts that look like men.

The Chinese evidently have some religious faith themselves.

In 1663, in England, a woman of 73, named Julia Cox, was indicted for changing herself into a hare. One Christian witness said that his dogs had started a hare near the old woman's home, and that, when the dogs ran it down, it changed into the woman herself. We read that in 1719 a Scotch woman, Margaret Nin-Gilbert, was indicted for witchcraft. A neighbor, William Montgomery, testified that he went home one night and found five cats by the fireside and a servant told him they were speaking among themselves. Later she admitted that she had been at Montgomery's house in the likeness of a cat, that Montgomery had broken her leg, either with his dt-trk or axe, and that the leg had since dropped off. She named other women who, she said, had been there with her in the form of cats, and declared the Devil had concealed them by raising a fog so that they could not be seen.

In parts of Russia it is still believed that Satan, in the form of a great serpent, carries off maidens. It is said that until very recently, if it does not persist to today, there was a custom in a certain French province to dress a big tomcat in swaddling clothes on Corpus Christi day and exhibit it in a gorgeous shrine. In 1875 a man living in Toulon told Berenger-Feraud that he had a friend who owned a wizard cat, which gave advice upon important matters by saying "Yes" or "No," and which disappeared at frequent intervals, when, its owner believed, it took human form.

But Satan's sorceries are not always confined to making wild beasts of humans. Perhaps he views the wild beasts that his competitor, Jehovah, ordains and crowns, and sits upon thrones, and the work disgusts him. Anyway, if the testimony of the Church is to be depended upon, Satan, at times, turns his attention to filling human brains with knowledge. Theologians assert that Satan does this in order to enjoy the sight of seeing the scholars he inspired thrown into foul dungeons, tortured, sometimes burned, and sometimes flayed alive by Jehovah's priests. But I doubt it. I think the pleasure is all Jehovah's and his priests. That is, if there really were a Jehovah. There is no doubt about the existence of the priests.

Did Satan inspire the brain of Bruno, just to see him suffer an agonizing death at the hands of the holy fathers? We are told that Bruno was burned to the glory of the God Jehovah, because Satan had filled him with knowledge and truth, which is contrary to the faith and teachings of Jehovah's religion, but there is no evidence offered to show that Satan could have been induced to light the fagots. The Church claims that it is Satan who has inspired the scientists and revolters against priestcraft and kingcraft. Is it not strange then that he should also bewitch people into wild beasts? Is there not reason to think that the holy fathers are mistaken, and that it is their own hell-and-damnation creed that has caused weak-minded people to go crazy and imagine themselves to be wolves and wildcats?

It appears that Satan, by filling heretics and rebels with knowledge and the love of freedom, equality and justice, is still waging the war he started in Heaven. Church history is full of the conflicts between Jehovah's divines and Satan's infidels. There was John Calvin, the father of Presbyterianism, and Michael Servetus, physician and student. Jehovah had no trouble in making a saint of Calvin, but was unable to hold Servetus in the faith. Satan got control of his brain, and Servetus began to think. This, as before mentioned, is contrary to Jehovah's religion. It is blasphemy, and, according to the divinely ordained laws given to Moses, is punishable by death. Servetus was tried at Vienne by the Roman Catholic Church, in 1553, convicted of heresy and condemned to be burned alive. With the help of some of Satan's wicked scholars, who managed to escape the claws of Jehovah's priests by keeping their mouths shut, Servetus made his escape and fled to Geneva, where John Calvin and his Protestant followers were in power. Servetus hoped for mercy among the new sect. He labored under the mistaken idea that Presbyterianism was more intelligent and liberty-loving than Catholicism. Calvin saw in Servetus, not a scholar, but a sinner, under the sorcery of Satan. Therefore he seized him in the name of his god, bound him in chains and locked him in a dungeon. The learned sinner was tried and convicted by the demented divine, and was burnt at the stake. It was a glorious victory of Jehovah over Satan.

Ingersoll's description of Calvin would seem to apply to the average orthodox preacher of to-day. He says:

> "Calvin was of a pallid, bloodless complexion, thin, sickly, irritable, gloomy, impatient, egotistic, tyrannical, heartless and infamous. He was a strange compound of revengeful morality, malicious forgiveness, ferocious charity, egotistic humility, and a kind of hellish justice. In other words, he was as near like the God of the Old Testament as his health permitted."

From the shriveled flesh and charred bones of Servetus, Jehovah and his hosts of Presbyterians marched forth to conquer Satan and his heretics. Presbyterianism tortured, hung and burned those who dared to think, with the same holy zeal of its Catholic mother. It carried on the war between Jehovah and Satan with all the ferocity of a true child of the faith. To again quote Ingersoll:

> "Liberty was banished from Geneva, and nothing but Presbyterianism was left. Honor, justice, mercy, reason and charity were all exiled; but the five points of predestination, particular redemption, irresistible grace, total depravity, and the certain perseverance of the saints remained instead. * * * The doctrines of Calvin spread rapidly, and were eagerly accepted by the multitudes on the continent, but Scotland, in a few years, became the real fortress of Presbyterianism. The Scotch succeeded in establishing the same kind of theocracy that flourished in Geneva. The clergy took possession and control of everybody and

everything. It is impossible to exaggerate the mental degradation, the abject superstition of the people of Scotland during the reign of Presbyterianism. Heretics were hunted and devoured as though they were wild beasts. The gloomy insanity of Presbyterianism took possession of a great majority of the people. They regarded their ministers as the Jews did Moses and Aaron. They believed that they were the special agents of God, and that whatsoever they bound in Scotland would be bound in Heaven. There was not one particle of intellectual freedom. No man was allowed to differ with the Church, or to even contradict a priest. Had Presbyterianism maintained its ascendancy, Scotland would have been peopled with savages today."

Satan and his thinkers had a narrow escape from utter extinction in Scotland. It has been wickedly suggested that if it had not been for Scotch whisky Scotland would have been completely saved.

One of the most devoted saints ever inspired by Jehovah was Thomas Torquemada, Inquisitor-General of Spain, born in 1420. At that time Satan, by his sorceries, had caused many to lose their faith in the Pope. He had planted the seeds of heresy in thousands of human brains.

Jehovah began to tremble at Satan's power. The world showed symptoms of becoming sane, and renouncing the orthodox religion. Jehovah succeeded in filling Torquemada to the limit with the holy faith, and turned him loose on Satan's heretics. Torquemada became the most valiant and victorious soldier of the cross recorded in history. He followed faithfully in the footsteps of his Lord, and made a record that almost, if not quite, equals Jehovah's own massacre and rape of the Midianites. Says Ernst Haeckel:

"Under the notorious Torquemada (1481-98), in Spain alone eight thousand heretics were burned alive and ninety thousand punished with the confiscation of their goods and the most grievous ecclesiastical fines; in the Netherlands, under the rule of Charles V, at least fifty thousand fell victims to the clerical bloodthirst."[i]

Torquemada did a good job. Spain has remained true to Jehovah to this day. Let Satan, through his sorceries, cause a scholar to appear in that Christian country, and his doom is sealed. Francisco Ferrer was shot to death by the same holy fathers that blessed the bloody work of Torquemada. Satan has tried every sorcery imaginable to puncture a hole in Jehovah's religion in Spain, but without avail. He once charmed a mouse to run out of a hole1 in a church wall and eat some of the sacrament that a priest had hocus-pocused into the actual body and blood of Christ. He evidently thought that the sight of a "varmint" devouring a son of God, without his father raising any rumpus about it, might somewhat jar the faith of the holy fathers. But it didn't. The priests knew it was Satan's work, and that Jehovah had remained quiet in order to test their faith. So they had the walls of the church torn down, captured a mouse, had it burned, and sprinkled the ashes on the altar.

Satan and his legions of devils take particular delight in frequenting the churches. They are present at every service. They fill the sanctified atmosphere with evil thoughts and suggestions. It was to frighten Satan and his devils away that church bells were introduced. They were sprinkled with holy water and blessed in the name of the Father, Son and Holy Ghost.

The Christian religion consists as much, if not more, in the fear of Satan, as it does in the love of Jehovah. All the affairs of men are influenced by these two spirits. Martin Luther, the founder of Protestantism, was much more concerned over Satan's sorceries than he was over Jehovah's tender mercies.

"The credulity which Luther manifested on all matters connected with diabolical intervention," says Lecky, "was amazing. * * * When

---

[i] Haekel, Ernst. The Riddle of the Universe.

speaking of witchcraft his language was emphatic and unhesitating. 'I would have no compassion on these witches,' he exclaimed, 'I would burn them all.'"

Again, speaking of Luther, Lecky says:

> "Satan became * * * the dominating conception of his life. In every critical event, in every mental perturbation, he recognized Satanic power. In the monastery of Wittenberg he constantly heard the Devil making a noise in the cloisters; and became at last so accustomed to the fact that he related that, on one occasion, having been awakened by the sound, he perceived that it was only the Devil, and accordingly went to sleep again. The black stain in the castle of Wartburg still marks the place where he flung an ink-bottle at the Devil. In the midst of his long and painful hesitation on the subject of transubstantiation (the turning of bread and wine into the actual body and blood of Christ), the Devil appeared to him and suggested a new argument."

It would seem that Satan had considerable to do with forming the Protestant creed. Maybe if he had been in sole charge of the job Protestantism would have been somewhat better and saner than it is.

A further description of Luther's faith in Satan's power is described as follows:

> "He told how an aged minister had been interrupted, in the midst of his devotions, by a devil who was grunting behind him like a pig. At Torgau, the Devil broke pots and basins, and flung them at the minister's head, and at last drove the minister's wife and servants half crazy out of the house. On another occasion, the Devil appeared in the law courts, in the character of a leading barrister, whose place he is said to have filled with the utmost propriety. Fools, deformed persons,

the blind and the dumb, were possessed by devils. Physicians, indeed, attempted to explain these infirmities by natural causes; but those physicians were ignorant men; they did not know all the power of Satan. Every form of disease might be produced by Satan, or by his agents, the witches; and none of the infirmities to which Luther was liable were natural, but his ear-ache was peculiarly diabolical."

Luther declared that Satan, like Jehovah, had the power to beget children by virgins, and that he did this quite often.

There is no account, however, of Satan having any of them crucified in order to appease his wrath at mankind.

It is recorded that Luther himself came in contact with one of these Satan-begotten children. Being a worshiper of Jehovah, Luther recommended that the child be thrown in the river.

The Catholics claim—and with considerable evidence in sight—that it was Luther's love of the fair sex that caused him to leave the mother church. Is it possible that he knew more about the parentage of that child than is told in the religious literature of the period?

That the war, started in Heaven, between Satan and Jehovah, is being still relentlessly carried on in this world, was firmly believed by Luther. It became the cornerstone of the Protestant creed. It is known as the doctrine of predestination. In this war man has no control over himself whatever. He is simply conscripted whether or no and must serve the god who gets him first.

"The human will," says Luther, "is like a beast of burden. If God mounts it, it wishes and goes as God wills; if Satan mounts it, it wishes and goes as Satan wills. Nor can it choose the rider it would prefer, or betake itself to him, but it is the riders who contend for its possession."

It is like the way the politicians have fixed it for us with their Democratic and Republican tickets.

"This is the acme of faith," declares Luther, "to believe that He is merciful who saves so few and who condemns so many; that He is just who at his own pleasure has made us necessarily doomed to damnation; so that, as Erasmus says, He seems to delight in the tortures of the wretched, and to be more deserving of hatred than of love."

This surely is, at Luther puts it, "the acme of faith." It certainly takes a strong stomach to love Jehovah. Luther sums it up in these words:

> "If by any effort of reason I could conceive how God could be merciful and just who shows so much anger and iniquity, there would be no need for faith."

That's the truth, even if a theologian did say it. No "effort of reason" can fathom it. It takes faith, and lots of it. Reason is a sin in the sight of Jehovah. It is inspired by Satan, and should be renounced by Christians. Once reason enters the brain of man, and overboard goes the whole orthodox structure—religion, social system, and all. Priests and princes, plutocrats and plunderers, landlords, joblords and warlords, all go tumbling into the junk pile when reason makes heretics and rebels out of superstitious slaves.

Luther believed in burning heretics and flaying rebels alive; he believed in the divine right of kings; he believed in witchcraft, slavery and polygamy; he believed in Jehovah, and his holy scriptures. Satan could not shake Luther's faith—he could not inject a spark of reason into the brain of Protestantism's founder. Luther walked the narrow path to the end, even as a blind pig works its passage through a dark alley—he was saved, not through any righteousness of his own, but because Jehovah had elected him to salvation before he was born.

Robert Burns has wittily portrayed such faith in "Holy Willie's Prayer":

> "O Thou that in the Heavens does dwell,
> Who, as it pleases best Thyself,
> Sends one to Heaven an' ten to Hell,

All for Thy glory,
And not for any good or ill
   They've done before Thee!

"I bless and praise Thy matchless might,
When thousands Thou has left in night,
That I am here before Thy sight,
   For gifts and grace
A burning and a shining light
   To all this place.

"What was I, or my generation,
That I should get such exaltation?
I, who deserv'd most just damnation
   For broken laws
Six thousand years ere my creation
   Thro' Adam's cause!

"When from my mother's womb I fell,
Thou might have plunged me deep in Hell
To gnash my gums, and weep, and wail
   In burning lakes,
Where damned devils roar and yell,
   Chain'd to their stakes.

"Yet I am here, a chosen sample,
To show Thy grace is great and ample;
I'm here a pillar o' Thy temple,
   Strong as a rock,
A guide, a buckler, and example

Satan and his Transformations

  To all Thy flock!

But for the unbeliever—

 "Lord, in Thy day o' vengeance try him!
 Lord, visit him who did employ him!
 And pass not in Thy mercy by them,
  Nor hear their pray'r,
 But for Thy people's sake destroy them,
  And do not spare!

 "But Lord, remember me and mine
 With mercies temporal and divine,
 That I for grace and wealth may shine
  Excell'd by none;
 And all the glory shall be Thine—
  Amen, Amen!"

Satan and his Transformations

5. Our Inspired Insanity

The demoralizing effect that the Christian myth exercises upon the minds of men and women is well nigh beyond comprehension. Ernst Haeckel truly says that it "lent its darkest character to the Middle Ages; it meant death to all freedom of mental life, decay to all science, corruption to all morality. From the noble height to which the life of the human mind had attained in classical antiquity, in the centuries before Christ and the first century after Christ, it soon sank, under the rule of papacy, to a level which, in respect of the knowledge of the truth, can only be termed barbarism. * * * It is impossible for us here to describe the pitiful retrogression of culture and morality during the twelve centuries of the spiritual despotism of Rome. It is very pithily expressed in a saying of the greatest and the ablest of the Hohenzollerns; Frederick the Great condensed his judgment in the phrase that the study of history led one to think that from Constantine to the date of the Reformation the whole world was insane."

Nor has that insanity yet passed away. Superstition still leads to slavery—faith to lunacy. Sane people would not be exploited by a capitalist class; they would not be led to war by plunderers; they would not be hypnotized by prostituted politicians; they would not believe the lies of press and pulpit; they would not be filled with devils.

The Christian New Testament teaches the existence of devils and witchcraft; it tells of Christ driving legions of devils out of a man and sending them into a herd of swine; it demands faith in these myths and absurdities. It also demands obedience to the powers that be.

Reviewing the history of what the Bible declares to be the "crime" of witchcraft, Lecky writes:

> "For more than fifteen hundred years it was universally believed that the Bible established, in the clearest manner, the reality of the crime, and that an amount of evidence, so varied and so ample as to preclude the very possibility of doubt, attested its continuance and its prevalence. The clergy denounced it with all the emphasis of authority. The legislators of almost every land enacted laws for its punishment. Acute judges, whose lives were spent in sifting evidence, investigated the question on countless occasions, and condemned the accused. Nations that were completely separated by position, by interests, and by character, on this one question were united. In almost every province of Germany, but especially in those where clerical influence predominated, the persecution raged with a fearful intensity. Seven thousand victims are said to have been burned at Treves, six hundred by a single bishop of Bamberg, and eight hundred in a single year in the bishopric of Wurtzburg. In France, decrees were passed on the subject by the Parliaments of Paris, Toulouse, Bordeaux, Rheims, Rouen, Dijon, and Rennes, and they were all followed by a harvest of blood. At Toulouse, the seat of the Inquisition, four hundred persons perished for sorcery at a single execution, and fifty at Douay in a single year. Remy, a judge of Nancy, boasted that he had put to death eight hundred witches in sixteen years. The executions that took place at Paris in a few months were, in the emphatic words of an old writer, 'almost infinite.' The fugitives who escaped to Spain were there seized and burned by the Inquisition. In that country the persecution spread to the smallest towns, and the belief was so deeply rooted in the popular mind, that a sorcerer was burnt as late as 1780. Torquemada devoted himself to the extirpation of witchcraft as zealously as to the extirpation of heresy, and he wrote

a book upon the enormity of the crime. In Italy, a thousand persons were executed in a single year in the province of Como; and in other parts of the country, the severity of the inquisitors at last created an absolute rebellion. The same scenes were enacted in the wild valleys of Switzerland and of Savoy. In Geneva, which was then ruled by a bishop, five hundred alleged witches were executed in three months; forty-eight were burnt at Constance or Ravensburg, and eighty in the little town of Valery, in Savoy. In 1670, seventy persons were condemned in Sweden, and a large proportion of them were burnt. And these are only a few of the more salient events in that long series of persecution which extended over almost every country, and continued for centuries with unabated fury. * * * In England the establishment of the Reformation was a signal for an immediate outburst of the superstition; and there, as elsewhere, its decline was represented by the clergy as the direct consequence and the exact measure of the progress of skepticism. In Scotland, where the Reformed ministers exercised greater influence than in any other country, and where the witch trials fell almost entirely into their hands, the persecution was proportionately atrocious. Probably the ablest defender of the belief was Glanvil, a clergyman of the English Establishment; and one of the most influential was Baxter, the greatest of the Puritans. It spread, with Puritanism, into the New World; and the executions in Massachusetts form one of the darkest pages in the history of America. The greatest religious leader of the last century (John Wesley) was among the latest of its defenders."

The boasted blessings the people have enjoyed under Christianity are a sight to behold. The heathen know nothing about them.

To further quote from Lecky:

"It may be stated, I believe, as an invariable truth, that, whenever a religion which rests in a great measure on a system of terrorism, and which paints in dark and forcible colors the misery of men and the power of evil spirits, is intensely realized, it will engender the belief in witchcraft or magic. The panic which its teachings will create, will overbalance the faculties of multitudes. The awful images of evil spirits of superhuman power, and of untiring malignity, will continually haunt the imagination."

At the time of this writing a notorious mountebank—a twentieth century mad bull of Calvinism—is being lavishly sugared by America's biggest profitmongers to hypnotize the masses into all the horrors of the Dark Ages. The Protestant churches are almost united in supporting this pulpiteer. His chief stock-in-trade is the Dark Age Devil and all his ancient sorceries. He preaches endless torment, and servility to the predatory powers that be, in one breath. At his ravings, we are told, thousands cringe in terror, begging to be saved. They kneel as of old before an avenging god, they tremble at the phantom picture of the old-time Satan, and they kiss the hands of the class that exploits them. They are religiously headed down the road to Yesterday.

"In all ages," says Ingersoll, "the people have honored those who dishonored them. They have worshiped their destroyers; they have canonized the most gigantic liars, and buried the great thieves in marble and gold. Under the loftiest monuments sleeps the dust of murder."

Faith in gods and devils is the foundation upon which faith in kings and capitalists rests; and the punishment inflicted by the gods upon heretics is worse than the sorceries of the devils; and, when carefully analyzed, it all works to the power and glory and profit of those who devour the people.

We are told of a famine that occurred in France in the eighth century, that God sent, said the priests, because the French people were behind in the payment of tithes to the church. Today we are told that God, not Satan, sends wars to punish us for our sins. Incidentally God sends immense profits along with the wars, that go into the pockets of the ones who stay at home and finance the "punishment."

On the other hand, Thomas Aquinas, who lived in the thirteenth century, assures us that Satan sends all tempests, diseases, and such like calamities. This same religious authority claimed that Satan frequently transported men and women through the air, and changed them into any shape he desired.

To again quote Lecky:

> "If any one ventured to deny that Satan possessed, or was likely to exercise this power, he was speedily silenced by a scriptural precedent. We read in the Old Testament that the Devil, by the divine permission, afflicted Job; and that among the means which he employed was a tempest which destroyed the house in which the sons of the patriarch were eating. The description, in the Book of Revelation, of the four angels who held the four winds, and to whom it was given to afflict the earth, was also generally associated with this belief; for, as St. Augustine tells us, the word angel is equally applicable to good or bad spirits. * * * Rain seems to have been commonly associated, as it still is in the Church of England, with the intervention of the Deity; but wind and hail were invariably identified with the Devil."

Satan, claimed St. Thomas Aquinas, carried Christ through the air to the pinnacle of the temple; and if he could do this, why couldn't he change an old woman into a wolf, or sail her over the moon? The prophet Habakkuk, so we are told, was once transported from Judea to Babylon; Philip the Evangelist once took a trip similar to this; and St. Paul aviated as far up as the third heaven.

The belief in witchcraft forms the very basis of Presbyterianism and Puritanism. Calvinism is composed of equal parts of Jehovah's salvation and damnation, and Satan's sorceries and scandals. Says Sir Walter Scott in his letters on "Demonology and Witchcraft:

> "On the whole, the Calvinists, generally speaking, were, of all the contending sects, the most suspicious of sorcery, the most undoubting believers in its existence, and the most eager to follow it up with what they conceived to be the due punishment of the most fearful crimes."

Of the reign of Presbyterianism in Scotland Lecky writes:

> "Supported by public opinion, the Scottish ministers succeeded in overawing all opposition, in prohibiting the faintest expression of adverse opinions, in prying into and controlling the most private concerns of domestic life; in compelling every one to conform absolutely to all the ecclesiastical regulations they enjoined; and in, at last, directing the whole scope and current of legislation. They maintained their ascendancy over the popular mind by a system of religious terrorism, which we can now barely conceive. (Much like the 'patriotic' terrorism maintained by the warlords.) The misery of man, the anger of the Almighty, the fearful power and continual presence of Satan, the agonies of Hell, were the constant subjects of their preaching. All the most ghastly forms of human suffering were accumulated as faint images of the eternal doom of the vast majority of mankind. Countless miracles were represented as taking place within the land, but they were almost all of them miracles of terror. Disease, storm, famine, every awful calamity that fell upon mankind, or blasted the produce of the soil, was attributed to the direct intervention of spirits; and Satan himself was represented as constantly appearing in a visible form upon the earth. Such teaching produced its natural effects. In a land where

credulity was universal, in a land where the intellect was numbed and palsied by these awful contemplations, where almost every form of amusement was suppressed, and where the thoughts of men were concentrated with an undivided energy on theological conceptions, such teaching necessarily created the superstition of witchcraft. Witchcraft was but one form of the panic it produced; it was but the reflection by a diseased imagination of the popular theology. We accordingly find that it assumed the most frightful proportions and the darkest characters. In other lands, the superstition was at least mixed with much of imposture; in Scotland it appears to have been entirely undiluted. It was produced by the teaching of the clergy, and it was everywhere fostered by their persecution. Eagerly, passionately, with a thirst for blood that knew no mercy, with a zeal that never tired, did they accomplish their task. Assembled in solemn synod, the college of Aberdeen, in 1603, enjoined every minister to take two of the elders of his parish to make 'a subtle and privy inquisition', and to question all the parishioners upon oath as to their knowledge of witches. Boxes were placed in the churches for the express purpose of receiving the accusations. When a woman had fallen under suspicion, the minister from the pulpit denounced her by name, exhorted his parishioners to give evidence against her, and prohibited anyone from sheltering her. In the same spirit, he exerted the power which was given him by a parochial organization, elaborated perhaps more skillfully than any other in Europe. Under these circumstances, the witch-cases seem to have fallen almost entirely into the hands of the clergy. They were the leading commissioners. Before them the confessions were taken. They were the acquiescing witnesses or the directors of the tortures by which those confessions were elicted."

The tragic story of Scotland, when completely in the clutches of the clergy, is told in Dalyell's "Darker Superstitions of Scotland." Also in Pitcairn's "Criminal Trials of Scotland" is found many of the original documents of the witch trials. We read:

> "The confessions were commonly taken before presbyteries, or certain special commissioners, who usually ranked among their number the leading clergy of those districts where their hapless victims resided."

Of the tortures inflicted by the Scotch Presbyterians to produce confessions, Lecky writes:

> "And when we read the nature of these tortures, which were worthy of an oriental imagination; when we remember that they were inflicted, for the most part, on old and feeble and half-doting women, it is difficult to repress a feeling of the deepest abhorrence for those men who caused and who encouraged them."

For my part, I do not try to repress such a feeling. I never pass by a Presbyterian church without experiencing the deepest abhorrence for all that it ever stood and still stands for. I was taught its monstrous doctrines when a child. Its frightfulness brought torture to my sensitive soul. When in later years, through honest research, I discovered the foul thing to be a lie, I learned to hate it, and I always will.

To continue with the account of the tortures:

> "If the witch was obdurate, the first, and it was said the most effectual, method of obtaining confession was by what was termed 'waking her.' An iron bridle or hoop was bound across her face with four prongs, which were thrust into her mouth. It was fastened behind to the wall by a chain, in such a manner that the victim was unable to lie down; and in this position she was sometimes kept for several days,

while men were constantly with her to prevent her from closing her eyes for a moment in sleep. Partly in order to effect this object, and partly to discover the insensible mark which was the sure sign of a witch, long pins were thrust into her body. At the same time, as it was a saying in Scotland that a witch would never confess while she could drink, excessive thirst was often added to her tortures."

It is recorded that some women endured this suffering for as long as five days and nights before they could be made to "confess;" and there is one case told of where the victim stood out for nine days and nights.

Pitcairn thus minutely describes the "witches' bridle":

"One of the most powerful incentives to confession was systematically to deprive the suspected witch of the refreshment of her natural sleep. * * * Iron collars, or witches' bridles, are still preserved in various parts of Scotland, which had been used for such iniquitous purposes. These instruments were so constructed that, by means of a hoop which passed over the head, a piece of iron having four points was forcibly thrust into the mouth, two of these being directed to the tongue and palate, the others pointing outward to each cheek. This infernal machine was secured by a padlock. At the back of the collar was fixed a ring, by which to attach the witch to a staple in the wall of her cell. Thus equipped, and night and day waked and watched by some skillful person appointed by her inquisitors, the unhappy creature, after a few days of such discipline, maddened by the misery of her forlorn and helpless state, would be rendered fit for confessing anything, in order to be rid of the dregs of her wretched life. At intervals fresh examinations took place, and these were repeated from time to time until her 'contumacy', as it was termed, was subdued. The clergy and kirk sessions appear to have been the unwearied instruments of 'purging the land of witchcraft;' and to them, in the first instance, all the complaints and informations were made."

What irony of fate, that women should be the chief supporters of the churches to this day!

If the witches' bridles failed to do the work, we read that "other and perhaps worse tortures were in reserve. The three principal that were habitually applied, were the pennywinkis, the boots, and the caschielawis. The first was a kind of thumb-screw; the second was a frame in which the leg was inserted, and in which it was broken by wedges, driven in by a hammer; the third was also an iron frame for the leg, which was from time to time heated over a brazier. Fire-matches (torches) were sometimes applied to the body of the victim."

Pitcairn tells of two cases, condemned in the same trial, in the year 1596, one of which was kept in "vehement tortour" for forty-eight hours in the "caschielawis." The other remained in the Presbyterian machine "for eleven days and eleven nights, whose legs were broken daily for fourteen days." Together with this the wretched victim of the Holy Bible that declares "thou shalt not suffer a witch to live" was scourged on the bare body until no particle of skin was left. We are told of the public sight of nine women burning in a bunch at Leith in 1664; of how, out of the kindness of the parsons' hearts, and for the sake of a merciful God, the witches were sometimes strangled before they were burned. But this was rarely the case. As a rule the reverends insisted on every agony imaginable. The Earl of Mar—who, it has been hinted, had but little regard for Jehovah's religion—relates how, "with a piercing yell, some women once broke half-burnt from the slow fire that consumed them, struggled for a few moments with despairing energy among the spectators, but soon with shrieks of blasphemy and wild protestations of innocence sank writhing in agony amid the flames."

Lecky relates a story, taken from a book called "The Secret Commonwealth," published in 1691, of a discussion a Scotch layman once had with his minister on the subject of old women turning themselves into cats. The minister said that he personally knew of one man that succeeded in cutting off the leg of a cat that attacked him, and that the cat's leg immediately turned into the leg of an old woman, and that four ministers signed a certificate attesting this to be a fact. As the book mentioned was written by a regularly ordained Presbyterian preacher, by the name of Robert Kirk, the story should not be questioned. It is also well to remember that the ancient theologians that compiled the larger part of the Bible were of the same intellectual calibre as the Presbyterian preacher that wrote that book. Nobody can reasonably doubt but that the story of the old woman and the cat's leg, and the story of Jonah riding in the belly of a whale, were inspired by the same sort of brains. It is impossible for a Christian to limit the power of Satan's sorceries or Jehovah's miracles. The early church associated the lily, as the symbol of purity, with pictures of the Virgin Mary. This soon started a religious notion that a virgin could become pregnant by eating lilies. There is no record in church history, however, of the plan succeeding. Why this is the case is hard to tell. A child born with a lily for a papa would add another feature to the world's religious wonders.

That Jehovah is on the side of tyranny, and Satan on the side of freedom, has never been disputed by the Church. Says Macaulay (Essays) : "The Church of England continued to be for more than 150 years the servile handmaid of monarchy, the steady enemy of public liberty. The divine right of kings and the duty of passively obeying all their commands were her favorite tenets. She held those tenets firmly through times of oppression, persecution and licentiousness, while the law was trampled down, while judgment was perverted, while the people were eaten as though they were bread."

A mouthpiece of the church declares: "Eternal damnation is prepared for all impenitent rebels in Hell with Satan the first founder of rebellion." "Heaven is the place of good obedient subjects, and Hell the prison and dungeon of rebels against God and prince." "A rebel is worse than the worst prince, and rebellion worse than the worst government of the worst prince hath hitherto been." Tyrants, we are told, are put in power to punish the people for their sins—"God placeth as well evil princes as good," therefore "for subjects to deserve through their sins to have an evil prince, and then to rebel against him, were double and treble evil by provoking God more to plague them."[i]

It appears that Jehovah has an irascible temper. If he sends a plague on the people, and the people rebel, he doubles the dose. Jehovah, not Satan, is the ordainer of all cruel and despotic laws. Did not the divinely inspired St. Paul command abject submission and obedience under Caligula, Claudius and Nero? Did not Martin Luther declare that a rebel against king or kaiser should be killed on sight? Did you ever hear of any orthodox Church authority advocating a revolution against oppression? Does not the Church bless the bloody wars that the rulers drive the people into? Are not the princes and profitmongers of the world pillars of the Church? Jehovah is the proclaimed god of the ruling and robbing classes. He is the god of the landlords, the joblords and warlords. Satan and his heretics are the rebels of earth.

The alleged sorceries and scandals of Satan appear as comedies when compared to the tragedies of Jehovah's savagery. In the gloomiest days of Church domination, when, for the entertainment of the people, "the glare and smoke of the fire of Hell were constantly exhibited, and piercing shrieks of agony broke upon the ear," the wicked and condemned comedians of the stage starred Satan in their plays. Says Lecky: "Satan was made to act the part of a clown. His appearance was greeted with shouts of laughter. He became at once the most prominent and most popular character of the piece, and was emancipated by virtue of his character from all restraints of decorum. One of the most impressive doctrines of the Church was thus indissolubly associated in the popular mind with the ridiculous, and a spirit of mockery and of satire began to play around the whole teaching of authority."

---

i   Homilies on Wilfull Rebellion and on Obedience

As to the position the Church maintained toward the theatre we read:

"The doctrine of the Church on this subject was clear and decisive. The theatre was unequivocally condemned, and all professional actors were pronounced to be in a condition of mortal sin, and were, therefore, doomed, if they died in their profession, to eternal perdition. This frightful proposition was enunciated with the most emphatic clearness by countless bishops and theologians, and was even embodied in the canon law and the rituals of many dioceses. The Ritual of Paris, with several others, distinctly pronounced that actors were by their very employment necessarily excommunicated. This was the sentence of the Church upon those whose lives were spent in adding to the sum of human enjoyments, in scattering the clouds of despondency, and charming away the weariness of the jaded mind. None can tell how many hearts it has wrung with anguish, or how many noble natures it has plunged into the depths of vice. As a necessary consequence of this teaching, the sacraments were denied to actors who refused to repudiate their profession, and, in France at least, their burial was as the burial of a dog. Among those who were thus refused a place in consecrated ground was the beautiful and gifted Le Couvreur, who had been perhaps the brightest ornament of the French stage. She died without having abjured the profession she adorned, and she was buried in a field for cattle upon the banks of the Seine. An ode by Voltaire, burning with the deep fire of an indignant pathos, has at once avenged and consecrated her memory."

What a dismal world this would be with nothing but the everlasting procession of Jehovah's saints!

All the joys and loves and laughter of life we owe to Satan's sinners. It is said that Jesus was their friend.

6. The Wonders of Christianity

Among other religious legends gathered by Frank Hamel in his *Human Animals* (1915), to which elaborate collection the writer acknowledges his indebtedness for many were-wolf tales, is that of a young nobleman of vicious habits named Jean de la Roque. St. Francis of Paula had the young man locked up in a monastery in order to reform him. In those days the clergy were endowed with the power of a czar. Roque became furious at this treatment, and beat day and night on the door of his cell, at the same time uttering loud cries of vengeance. At last he became utterly exhausted and lay down on the floor and fell into a profound sleep. Then, we are told, St. Francis entered the cell, and, waking the young sinner, said to him, "How now, friend, what thinkest thou? Pull from thine ear that which torments thee so." Roque, half unconscious, did as he was told; he stuck his finger in his right ear and pulled out a monstrous hairy worm. Then he stuck his finger in the other ear and pulled out another worm of the same sort. They were devils, put in there by Satan. Thus relieved of the evil spirits, Jean de la Roque forsook his wicked ways and became a holy monk.

The miraculous power that the saints had over all kinds of animals is vouched for by the same sort of au-thprities that canonized the Scriptures.

We are told that "St. Gentius made a wolf which had eaten one of his oxen help him with the plowing." Another saint, by the name of Maidoc, was so poor that he owned neither ox, nor horse, nor ass; so he ordered a sea-cow to come out of the ocean, which she did, and he had her do his plowing. St. Regulus, an archbishop of Aries and Senlis, was once about to cast a devil out of a man, just as Jesus is reputed to have done; only, instead of sending the devil into a pig, St. Regulus proposed to send it into an ass standing by. It seems that this particular devil was aware of the intelligence that asses sometimes possess. He had probably heard of the story of Balaam. Anyway, say the religious records of the case, the devil urged St. Regulus to find some other animal to send him into. But St. Regulus paid no attention to the devil's request. He pronounced his holy hocus pocus, and the devil was immediately driven out of the man, and was about to enter the ass, as the saint had commanded, when the ass stretched forth his fore-foot and drew the sign of the cross on the ground; whereupon the devil flew in terror back to Hell.

The sign of the cross was something that Satan and his imps could not stand. Also consecrated bread and wine threw the legions of Hell into spasms.

Samuel Harsnett, in his *Popish Impostures*, relates the story of Simon Magus, a wizard of the period, sending the Apostle Peter a pack of devils in the form of dogs for the purpose of devouring him. St. Peter, "not looking for such currish guests, consecrates certain morsels of bread and throws them to the dog-devils, and by the power of that bread they are all put to flight."

Satan had evidently failed to warn Simon Magus that St. Peter, under the spell of Jehovah, was some wizard himself. The fifth chapter of the Acts of the Apostles discloses Peter's supernatural powers; we are told therein that he suddenly killed a man and his wife because they made some misrepresentations concerning a certain real estate transaction. The warlords of today would give anything for an army of St. Peters.

When St. Stanislaus Kostka was about to join the order of Jesuits, Satan caused a severe sickness to overtake him. He further appeared to the saint in the form of a big black dog, and, flying at his throat, tried to strangle him. But Stanislaus did not lose his presence of mind; he made the sign of the cross, and Satan fled.

The utter insanity that can be produced by religious superstition is disclosed by the words of Frank Hamel. He says:

"In the Middle Ages witches who were condemned to the stake, confessed to having taken the shapes of cats, hares, dogs, horses, and many other animals, being prompted to such changes by the Devil, with whom they were in league."

Whether these self-confessed witches were insane before being accused of witchcraft or whether part, or even all of them, were driven iinsane by the horrible tortures used at the trials to extort confession, is a matter of conjecture; but this is certain—the priests and preachers, and the Christian judges, were madmen—mad as the savage that wrote the scriptural law in the mouth of a god, "Thou shalt not suffer a witch to live."

Superstition is an insanity of degrees. A person afflicted with only a small amount of it may appear tolerably sane; full faith in the Bible requires complete madness.

Dr. John Webster, in his work called *The Displaying of Supposed Witchcraft*, published in 1677, tells of a witch trial that took place at Lancaster, England, in the year 1663. A half-witted boy of eleven years—a promising candidate for holy orders—by the name of Edmund Robinson, "son of Edmund Robinson of Pendle forest," was the principal witness in the case. We read that he appeared before Richard Shuttleworth and John Starkey, Justices of the Peace, "who upon oath informeth, being examined concerning the great meeting of the witches of Pendle, saith that upon All Saints-day last past, he, this informer being with one Henry Parker a near door-neighbor to him in Wheatley Cave, desired the said Parker to give him leave to gather some bulloes, which he did. In gathering whereof he saw two greyhounds, namely a black and a brown; one came running over the next field towards him, he verily thinking the one of them to be Mr. Nutter's and the other to be Mr. Robinson's, the said gentlemen then having suchlike. And saith the said greyhounds came to him, and fawned on him, they having about their necks either of them a collar, unto which was tied a string: which collars (as this informant afirmeth) did shine like gold. And he was thinking that some either of Mr. Nutter's or Mr. Robinson's family should follow them, yet seeing nobody to follow them, he took the same greyhounds thinking to course with them. And presently a hare did rise very near before him. At the sight whereof he cried 'Loo, Loo, Loo,' but the dogs would not run. Whereupon he being very angry took them with the strings that were about their collars, tied them to a little bush at the next hedge, and, with a switch that he had in his hand, he beat them. And instead of the black greyhound Dickenson's wife stood up, a neighbor whom this informer knoweth. And instead of the brown one a little boy whom this informer knoweth not. At which sight this informer being afraid, endeavored to run away; and being stayed by the woman, namely Dickenson's wife, she put her hand into her pocket, and pulled forth a piece of silver much like to a fair shilling, and offered to give it to him to hold his tongue and not tell: which he refused saying, 'Nay, thou art a witch.' Whereupon she put her hand into her pocket again, and pulled out a thing like unto a bridle that jingled, which she put on the little boy's head; which said boy stood up in the likeness of a white horse, and in the brown greyhound's stead. Then immediately Dickenson's wife took the informer before her upon the said horse and carried him to a new house called Hearthstones, being about a quarter of a mile off."

There, we are told, the boy was witness to "a feast of the witches." His father finally became worried at the boy's absence, and at last, so he declared, found him wandering in the forest "so affrighted and distracted that he neither knew his father; nor did he know where he was, and so continued nearly a quarter of an hour before he came to himself, when he told the above curious happenings."

We are told that "the seventeen Pendle forest witches condemned in Lancashire obtained a reprieve and were sent to London, where they were examined by His Majesty himself and the Council."

Orthodox Christians used to believe that a man could be transformed into a horse by a witch throwing a magic halter over his head while he was asleep in bed. Then the witch would mount him, and ride to the witches' tryst. This was successfully worked for years by the witches, until one of them, one night, not being able to locate an ordinary man asleep in bed, tried her enchantment upon a monk. The monk turned into a horse all right, and the witch jumped on his back; not, however, before the monk, feeling the spell of Satan coming over him, had hurriedly made the sign of the cross. This brought Jehovah at once to his aid, who inspired him what to do; he should slip the bridle off his own head and throw it over the head of the rider. This, with Jehovah's help, the monk managed to do, whereupon he immediately became a monk again, and the witch became a mare. The holy man of God mounted her and leisurely rode back to the monastery. What then became of the mare is unknown. All we know is that Satan helped her to make a get-away. However, the story became widespread, so that afterwards it was no uncommon thing for men bewitched into a horse to turn the trick upon their rider in the manner prescribed by the monk.

The fate that overtook a witch at Yarrowfoot, England, who was turned into a mare by the man she had bewitched, is one of the most wonderful miracles in church history. The man not only rode the witch-mare, but also had her shod and then sold her to her own husband. In order to maintain the enchantment he had left the magic bridle on her. When her husband removed the bridle, Jehovah removed the enchantment; and one can imagine the husband's surprise and consternation as the mare all of a sudden turned into his wife, with the horseshoes still nailed to her hands and feet.

A similar miracle, and just as wonderful, if not more so, as the foregoing, runs as follows: A farmer living near Ostrel, Denmark, had a hired-hand, who, no matter how much he ate, became thinner and thinner every day. The wife of the farmer was a good cook, and loaded the table with wholesome food, and always insisted on the hungry hired-hand eating his fill. But it did no good. It seemed that the more he devoured the scrawnier he became. Finally, becoming alarmed at his condition, he went to a priest. The priests, following New Testament instructions, were the family physicians at that time.

After carefully looking the hired-hand over, the holy father made the sign of the cross and thereby got into communication with Jehovah. Jehovah then diagnosed the case, and declared the farmer's wife to be a witch of Satan, who every night, when all the household were sound sleep, transformed the hired-hand into a horse, and rode him from Ostrel, Denmark, to Troms Church, Norway, and back again; so it was not to be wondered at that the poor fellow was growing thinner and weaker every day.

With this knowledge at hand the priest went to his medicine chest and gave the hired-hand some magic ointment, and told him to rub it on his head at night, and it would produce a violent itching, that would not only awaken him at the proper time, but would also, on account of the itching, cause him to break the enchantment. The man went back to the farm and followed the priest's directions. It worked fine. He awoke in the middle of night, and found himself standing by the church with the magic bridle in his hand, which he had torn off while scratching his head. Jehovah knew that was just what would happen. All around him stood witch-horses, tied together by each other's tails, that had been ridden by witches to the midnight worship of Satan. Finally his mistress came out of the church and walked up to him, and, discovering the transformation that had taken place, cast a friendly look at him and started to take the bridle from his hand and throw it over his head again. But the hired-hand was too quick for her. He threw the bridle over her own head, whereupon she immediately became a mare, which he mounted, and started for home.

Now this hired hand had a mind for business, and, noting the fine appearance of the animal he was riding, he began to figure how to profit by the good fortune that had befallen him; so he rode along the way in a leisurely manner, until morning appeared, and then hunted a blacksmith and had the mare shod. He finally reached home about noon, and told his master that he had been away making a purchase of the fine mare he was riding, which, he said, he was willing to sell at a fair price. The result was that the master paid a pretty stiff price for the mare and led her to the barn; but when he removed her bridle, and was about to put a halter on her, there stood his wife, shod hand and foot. Being a good Christian, he ran her off the place, and she never came back.

Like all other religious superstitions, Satan's witchcraft was a money-maker. Not only was the property of a condemned witch confiscated and divided among the informers and persecutors, but religious detectives made an easy living running down witches. These detectives were called "witch-finders." Their business had the sanction of Jehovah of the Old Testament.

One Matthew Hopkins, of Manningtree, Essex, England, was a notorious witch-finder of the seventeenth century. He was paid 20 shillings by each town wherein he ran down a witch. As there were no lunatic asylums in those days, nor institutions for imbeciles, and as the Christian creed had overrun the country with idiots, it was an easy matter to discover a number of witches in every burg. Any old, toothless woman would do; and any superstitious, feeble-minded, over-religious, gibbering bumpkin would answer for a witness.

With all our boasted enlightenment and advancement, it would not be a very hard matter, in some localities, to again start a witch-craze. It is no more crazy than a war-craze. A large part of the masses can still be driven bughouse at the command of moneylords and clergy, of politicians and their prostituted press.

In 1644 this Matthew Hopkins was commissioned by the British Parliament to make a general circuit of the country for the discovery of witches. He traveled for three years, in company with several boon companions. They were of the same pattern as secret service men. We are told that they had "sixteen persons hanged at Yarmouth, forty at Bury, and at least sixty in other parts of Suffolk, Norfolk and Huntingdonshire."

At a trial of witches at Chelmsford, in 1645, Hopkins made a deposition against one Elizabeth Clarke, "who confessed that she had known the Devil intimately for more than six years and that he visited her between three and five times a week. She invited Hopkins and his companions, one of whom was a man called Sterne, to stay at her house for a time until she could call up one of her white imps for them to see. Presently there appeared on the scene an imp like a dog, white and with sandy spots, which seemed to be very fat and plump, with short legs. The animal forthwith vanished away. The said Elizabeth gave the name of this imp as Jarmara. And immediately afterward there appeared another imp, which she called Vinegar Tom, in the shape of a greyhound with long legs. The said Elizabeth then remarked that the next imp should be black in color and that it should come for Master Sterne (the other witness already mentioned), and it appeared as she promised, but presently vanished without leaving a sign. The last imp of all to come before the spectators was a creature in the shape of a polecat, but the head somewhat bigger. The said Elizabeth then disclosed to the informant that she had five imps of her own. And two other imps with which she had dealings belonged to a certain Beldame Anne West."

On such testimony as this, weak-minded old women were tortured, hung and burned. The Church and courts accepted the words of lunatics and liars. When rational men remonstrated against the outrage, they were hounded as blasphemers against God and traitors to the king. Nor is it difficult to note a likeness to this mania, even to this day.

7. Enchantments, Transformations and Familiar Spirits

The belief in enchantments, transformations, and those having familiar spirits, has been universal among all races. They all have their deities and demons, Jehovahs and Satans. It is mostly the followers of the Bible, however, that torture and put to death those charged with Satan's sorceries. It is the Christians that burn "witches" and heretics.

It is charged that the North American Indians tortured, and even killed, Roman Catholic missionaries. These are held up as martyrs to the Christian faith. But the facts in the case are that the Indians did not torture and kill these priests on account of their religion, but because Protestant preachers, coming later, told the Indians that the Catholic priests were devils, sent by Satan to drag them down to Hell.

The Indians had never heard of such a fearful place as Hell, or such a fearful god as Jehovah, who sends unbelievers there, until the Christians came along. Once filled with the Christian faith, they naturally became as mad as the Christians themselves.

The legend of Circe, made immortal in Homer's "Odyssey," comes down, to us from the folk-lore and fairy tales of the ancient world. Circe was the daughter of Helios and the ocean nymph Perse, and was famed for her skill in magic. She married a prince of Colchis, and then killed him in order to obtain his kingdom. For this the subjects of the prince drove her out of the land.

If they had been orthodox Christians, and Circe had been accused of turning the prince into a horse and riding him through the night to a witches' prayermeeting, Circe would have been tortured and burned, according to Jehovah's commands; but, being heathen, they merely banished her out of sight for the crime of manslaughter.

With the help of her father Circe reached the Island of Aea, off the coast of Italy, and there set up her magic court. Ulysses, on a returning voyage from the Trojan War, stopped at Aea, where his companions were enticed and feasted by the enchantress. Provisions had ran short on the ship, and they were hungry and thirsty, and gave way to excess. Circe served them with a magic drink, that transformed them into swine.

A liberal rendering of the legend is found in "The Story of the Odyssey," People's Edition. Eurylochus and his companions found Circe's palace in an open space in a wood, and Ulysses had the following account from the lips of Eurylochus:

> "All about were wolves and lions, yet these harmed not the men, but stood up on their hind-legs, fawning upon them, as dogs fawn upon their master when he comes from his meal, because he brings the fragments with him that they love. And the men were afraid. And they stood in the porch and heard the voice of Circe as she sang with a lovely voice and plied the loom. Then said Polites (who was dearest of all his comrades to Ulysses), 'Someone within plies a loom, and sings with a loud voice. Some goddess is she, or woman. Let us make haste and call.' So they called to her, and she came out and beckoned to them that they should follow. And she bade them sit, and mixed for them a mess, red wine, and in it barley meal and cheese and honey, and mighty drugs withal, of which, if a man drank, he forgot all that he loved. And when they had drunk she smote them with her wand. And

lo! they had of a sudden the heads and the voices and the bristles of swine, but the heart of a man was in them still. And Circe shut them in sties, gave them mast and acorns and cornel to eat."

But Ulysses did not come under the spell of Circe's enchantment. The god Hermes had provided him with an herb called moly, that made him immune from all sorceries. He made love to the charming Circe, and was accepted, and he demanded that his companions be restored to their original shape. To this Circe complied. Ulysses lived with the enchantress for a year, and then sailed away. Circe instructed him how to sail to the land of shades, where he could learn his future fate from the prophet Teiresias.

The pagan gods and goddesses perform as many wonders as the Christian deities and demons. Circe was the daughter of a sea-nymph. Isn't that as wonderful as being born of a virgin?

Only, had some sailor of a hundred or so years ago returned from wandering the seas, to his Christian home, and told a tale as pagans tell of Circe, holy inquisitors would have been sent to. discover the abode of the sorceress; and, did they perchance find a shore where dwelt some elderly women, there would be a burning of witches in the name of the Bible god.

The ancient Greeks, not being Christians, turned the legend into classic lore.

It was only through an oversight that Homer's beautiful poem was not destroyed by the early priests of the Church. They tried to burn up every book but the Bible. They tried to cover the earth with a blanket of ignorance.

The people of the Polynesian islands tell stories of women who have given birth to animals. Sometimes they have twins, one a human and one a beast. It is related that a native of New Guinea once told a Christian missionary that an ancestress of his had given birth to a boy and also to an iguana. The missionary laughed at such nonsense, and then preached a sermon to the heathen in which he declared that if the heathen did not believe that a virgin gave birth to a god they would all go to Hell.

A story somewhat similar to that of the New Guinea woman that gave birth to an iguana is told by the Mussulmans concerning Eve. In the Book Al Araf, in the Koran, we read that Eve "called upon God their Lord, saying, If thou give a child rightly shaped, we will surely be thankful." The Mohammedan commentators explain this passage as follows:

> "When Eve was big with her first child, the Devil came to her and asked her whether she knew what she carried within her, and which way she should be delivered of it, suggesting that possibly it might be a beast. She, being unable to give an answer to this question, went in a fright to Adam, and acquainted him with the matter, who, not knowing what to think of it, grew sad and pensive. Whereupon the Devil appeared to her again (or, as others say, to Adam), and pretended that he by his prayers would obtain of God that she might be safely delivered of a son in Adam's likness, provided they would promise to name him Abda'lhareth, or the servant of al Hareth (which was the Devil's name among angels), instead of Abd'allah, or the servant of God, as Adam had designed. This proposal was agreed to, and accordingly, when the child was born, they gave it the name, upon which it immediately died."[i]

H. A. Giles, in his [translation of] *Strange Stories from a Chinese Studio*, (1880) tells of a traveler arriving at a public house in Yang-Chow accompanied by donkeys. He told the landlord to put the donkeys in the stable, but under no circumstances to let them have any water. The traveler then went away for a short time. In the meanwhile the donkeys made such a racket in the stable, and became

---

i   *Al Koran*, English translation of George Sale (1734), appendix, page 492.

so restless, that the landlord turned them loose; upon which they ran to a pond nearby, and began to drink. But the water had hardly touched their lips, when the five donkeys turned into five young women. Not knowing what to do, the landlord escorted the young women into the house and hid them.

About this time the traveler returned, leading five sheep. These, also, were turned over to the landlord, with the request that he shut them in the stable with the donkeys. But the landlord's suspicions, as well as his curiosity, was so aroused that he led the sheep immediately to water. No sooner did they begin to drink, than they turned into young men.

The story of "Aladdin and His Wonderful Lamp" is based on Chinese legends of sorcery. If the canonizers of the Bible had been Chinese, the Book of Aladdin would doubtless appear as an inspired work.

Here is a miracle, narrated by William McCulloch in his *Bengali Household Tales*, alleged to be performed by a heathen Hindu, as wonderful as anything ever performed by Jehovah or Satan:

A Hindu fakir, or yogi, removes a stone from an underground passage, and descending therein he comes back bringing a monkey. He then plucks a few leaves from a tree nearby, gets a bucket of water, throws the leaves in the water, communes a minute with a Hindu god or devil, then pours the water on the monkey. The monkey then immediately turns into a beautiful maiden. The fakir takes her by the hand, and with her descends again into the underground passage. Early the next morning the two re-appear, when the fakir mixes some more leaves and water, pours it over the maiden, and she becomes a monkey again.

What's the use of sending missionaries to tell these people about the whale swallowing Jonah?

Herodotus, the Greek historian, who is called "The Father of History," says that the ancient Egyptians were the first to teach the immortality of the soul. They claimed that when the body dies the soul enters the form of an animal that is born at that minute, and that it passes on from one animal into another, until it has gone through the various forms and existences of all life, whether of earth, water, or air, and then it enters again into a human body. All these incarnations require three thousand years.

Pythagoras taught the transmigration of souls, and Empedocles said he had passed through many forms of animal life.

Frank Hamel, in his *Human Animals*, quotes Shakespeare's "Midsummer Night's Dream," where "Puck is gifted with the power of transformation."

> "Sometimes a horse I'll be, sometimes a hound,
> A hog, a headless bear, sometimes a fire,
> And neigh, and bark, and grunt, and roar, and burn
> Like horse, hound, hog, bear, fire, at every turn."

Puck also had the power to transform others into animals. He turned Bottom into an ass.

Charles Lamb, in his "Essays of Elia," writes:

> "Gorgons and Hydras, and Chimaeras — dire stories of Celaeno and the Harpies, may reproduce themselves in the brain of superstition— but they were there before.
>
> They are transcripts, types—the archetypes are in us, and eternal. How else should the recital of that which we know in a waking sense to be false, come to affect us at all?—or
>
> Names whose sense we see not,
> Fray us with things that be not?
>
> Is it that we naturally conceive terror from such objects, considered in their capacity of being able to inflict upon us bodily injury?— O, least of all! These terrors are of older standing. They date beyond the body—or, without the body, they would have been the same. All

the cruel, tormenting, defined devils in Dante—tearing, mangling, choking, stifling, scorching demons—are they one-half so fearful to the spirit of a man, as the simple idea of a spirit unembodied following him:

> Like one that on a lonesome road
> Doth walk in fear and dread,
> For having once turn'd round, walks on,
> And turns no more his head;
> Because he knows a frightful fiend
> Doth close behind him tread.

That the kind of fear here treated is purely spiritual— that it is strong in proportion as it is objectless on earth —and that it predominates in the period of sinless infancy—are difficulties the solution of which might afford some probable insight into our ante-mundane condition, and a peep at least into the shadowland of pre-existence."

The doctrine of transmigration has been accepted and taught by many of the world's philosophers. Theosophy teaches reincarnation. So do the followers of Buddha. But these teachings contain no horrors, no degrading influence on the mind. In fact, they all point to a spiritual evolution reaching toward perfection.

With Christianity it is different. The lost souls are doomed for all eternity. In the Christian Hell there is no hope. It is the foulest faith on earth. It takes the legends, the fairy tales, the race memories, and turns them into a diabolism of everlasting, unutterable torture.

The Christian creed, under the supervision of the Roman tyrant, Constantine, was cunningly constructed to frighten the slaves into submission. The injunction of the Pharisee, Paul, commanding slaves to obey their masters, and subjects to be submissive to the God-ordained powers that be, with the threat of eternal damnation to rebels, has, for centuries, cursed the Christian world with masters and menials, plutocrats and paupers, and bloody wars.

Robert G. Ingersoll, in a lecture delivered in 1884, spoke these words—words carrying even a deeper meaning than when spoken:

> "How many millions of Christians are now armed and equipped to destroy their fellow-Christians? Who are the men in Europe crying against war? Who wishes to have the nations disarmed? Is it the Church? No; the men who do not believe in what they call this religion of peace. When there is a war, and when they make a few thousand widows and orphans; when they strew the plain with dead patriots, Christians assemble in their churches and sing 'Te Deum Laudamus.' Why? Because he has enabled a few of his children to kill some others of his children. This is the religion of peace—the religion that invented the Krupp gun, that will hurl a ball weighing two thousand pounds through twenty-four inches of solid steel. This is the religion of peace that covers the sea with men-of-war, clad in mail, in the name of universal forgiveness. This is the religion that drills and uniforms millions of men to kill their fellows."

Satan, with all his sorceries, never led the Christians in war. The Christian nations all look to Jehovah as they go to battle. They never pray to Satan to help them slaughter. They all pray to Jehovah to assist them in the bloody work. No chaplains of Satan accompany the regiments. They are all chaplains of Jehovah. The powers that be, that drive the masses to war, are all followers of Jehovah.

> "Let every soul be subject unto the higher powers. For there is no power but of God; the powers that be are ordained of God."

Satan is not responsible for a single sceptered scoundrel.

"Whosoever therefore resisteth the power, resisteth the ordinance of God; and they that resist shall receive to themselves damnation."

"He that believeth not shall be damned."

These infamous threats have been thundered into the ears of the plundered people for nearly two thousand years; they have covered the earth with madness and murder.

In contrast, listen to the voice of the heathen Buddha:

"Never will I seek nor receive private individual salvation; never enter into the final peace alone; but forever and everywhere will I live and strive for the universal redemption of every creature throughout all worlds. Never will I leave this world of sin and sorrow and struggle until all are delivered. Until then, I will remain and suffer where I am."

The teachings of this gentle heathen never inspired the building of frightful engines of death. They do not demand the torture and killing of heretics; they have burned no scholars at the stake; they have put to death no witches. The Christians have robbed and ravished them. They have suffered beyond words at the hands of Christian warlords.' Their lands have been stolen from them by Christian thieves. But they have kept their souls clean. Maybe, after all, there is something in this.

Against the craven, Christian threat of eternal damnation, the great soul of Ingersoll hurled the most terrific indictment:

"Eternal Pain!

"All the meanness of which the heart of man is capable is in that one word—Hell.

"That word is a den, a cave, in which crawl the slimy reptiles of revenge.

"That word certifies to the savagery of primitive man.

"That word is the depth, the dungeon, the abyss, from which civilized man has emerged.

"That word is the disgrace, the shame, the infamy of our revealed religion.

"That word fills all the future with the shrieks of the damned.

"That word brutalizes the New Testament, changes the Sermon on the Mount to hypocrisy and cant, and pollutes and hardens the very heart of Christ.

"That word adds an infinite horror to death, and makes the cradle as terrible as the coffin.

"That word is the assassin of joy, the mocking murderer of hope. That word extinguishes the light of life and wraps the world in gloom. That word drives reason from his throne, and gives the crown to madness.

"That word drove pity from the hearts of men, stained countless swords with blood, lighted fagots, forged chains, built dungeons, erected scaffolds, and filled the world with poverty and pain.

"That word is a coiled serpent in the mother's breast, that lifts its fanged head and hisses in her ear:—Your child will be the fuel of eternal fire.'

"That word blots from the firmament the star of hope and leaves the heavens black.

"That word makes the Christian's God an eternal torturer, an everlasting inquisitor—an infinite wild beast.

"This is the Christian prophecy of the eternal future :

"No hope in Hell.

"No pity in Heaven.

"No mercy in the heart of God."

And who wrote that word? Theologians of the same mental calibre as those that for centuries swore that old women, with the help of Satan, could turn themselves into wolves and wildcats. Doctors of divinity of the same mental calibre that tortured and burned heretics and witches. Doctors of divinity of the same mental calibre that fawn on the exploiters and extortioners that prey upon the world's workers. Doctors of divinity of the same mental calibre—the same madness—that bless the bloody wars of the world's ruling classes.

These doctors of divinity do not charge Satan with constructing Hell. According to their inspired records there is no reason to think that Satan knew anything about the place until Jehovah and his legions tumbled him over the walls of Paradise. The doctors of divinity acknowledge the God Jehovah as the sheriff of Hell. It is he that plunges lost souls into burning brimstone. It is he—the God Jehovah—that commands obedience to the world's brigands and butchers. Satan is guiltless of these things. Some of the early Christians, that taught that Jehovah of the Jews was an evil spirit, whom Christ had come to destroy, appear to have had good grounds for their doctrine.

8. Where Did Satan Come From?

In Ingersoll's lecture on "The Devil" the question comes up: "Now, where did the idea that a Devil exists come from? How was it produced?"

And the answer is:

> "Fear is an artist—a sculptor— a painter. All tribes and nations, having suffered, having been the sport and prey of natural phenomena, having been struck by lightning, poisoned by weeds, overwhelmed by volcanoes, destroyed by earthquakes, believed in the existence of a Devil, who was the king — the ruler — of innumerable smaller devils, and all these devils have been from time immemorial regarded as the enemies of men. * * * A man walking in the woods at night— just a glimmering of the moon—everything uncertain and shadowy—sees a monstrous form. One arm is raised. His blood grows cold, his hair lifts. In the gloom he sees the eyes of an ogre—eyes that flame with malice. He feels that the something is approaching. He turns, and with a cry of horror takes to his heels. He is afraid to look back. Spent, out of breath, shaking with fear, he reaches his hut and falls at the door. When he regains consciousness, he tells his story and, of course, the children believe. When they become men and women they tell father's story of having seen the Devil to their children, and so the children

and grandchildren not only believe, but think they know, that their father — their grandfather — actually saw a devil.

"An old woman sitting by the fire at night—a storm raging without—hears the mournful sough of the wind. To her it becomes a voice. Her imagination is touched, and the voice seems to utter words. Out of these words she constructs a message or a warning from the unseen world. If the words are good, she has heard an angel; if they are threatening and malicious, she has heard a devil. She tells this to her children and they believe. They say that mother's religion is good enough for them. A girl suffering from hysteria falls into a trance— has visions of the infernal world. The priest sprinkles holy water on her pallid face, saying: 'She hath a devil.' A man utters a terrible cry; falls to the ground; foam and blood issue from his mouth; his limbs are convulsed. The spectators say: 'This is the Devil's work.'

"Through all the ages people have mistaken dreams and visions of fear for realities. To them the insane were inspired; epileptics were possessed of devils; apoplexy was the work of an unclean spirit. For many centuries people believed that they had actually seen the malicious phantoms of the night, and so thorough was this belief—so vivid—that they made pictures of them. They knew how they looked. They drew and chiseled their hoofs, their horns—all their malicious deformities. * * * The people believed that Hell was their native land; that the Devil was a king, and that he and his imps waged war against the children of men."

Sometimes people worshiped a bad Devil instead of a good God. They feared the Devil, but had perfect confidence that the God would do them no harm, so worship and sacrifice were unnecessary so far as he was concerned. They were like the little boy whose mother, one night, caught him jumping into bed without saying his customary prayers.

"Why, Johnnie," she exclaimed, "have you forgotten your prayers?"

"No, mamma," he replied, "but I didn't say any last night, nor the night before, nor the night before that, and I ain't going to say any tonight nor tomorrow night. And then if nothin' happens I'm going to quit altogether."

The devils of one tribe were often the gods of another, and vice versa; and the cast-off, degraded gods of one people frequently became the devils of another.

The Devil has been represented in the form of a serpent among many different races. It was in this form that he appeared to Eve. Serpent worship has been the religion of different peoples in different parts of the world. The Mohammedan gospel of Barnabas says that the sentence that Jehovah pronounced upon the serpent for appearing as Satan in the Garden of Eden was that he should have his legs cut off by the angel Michael, with the sword that Jehovah carried himself; and that Satan, for appearing in the shape of a serpent, and rendering our first parents unclean, was condemned to eat human excrements for all eternity. Mohammedan writers assert that the serpent that Moses transformed from the rod, that devoured the serpents of the Egyptian magicians, was an enormous devil. They say that "he was hairy, and of so prodigious a size, that when he opened his mouth his jaws were fourteen cubits asunder, and when he laid his lower jaws on the ground, his upper jaws reached to the top of Pharaoh's palace; that Pharaoh seeing this monster making toward him, fled from it, and was so terribly frightened that he befouled himself; and that the whole assembly also betaking themselves to their heels, no less than twenty-five thousand of them lost their lives in the press."

Another interesting item, concerning Adam, that is vouched for by the Mussulmans, has, for some reason, been overlooked by the Christians. They claim that "God stroked Adam's back, and extracted from his loins his whole posterity, which should come into the world until the resurrection, one generation after another; that these men were actually assembled all together in the shape of small ants, which were endued with understanding; and that after they had, in the presence of the angels, confessed their dependence on God, they were again caused to return to the loins of their great ancestor."

Can any one doubt the inspiration of the Mohammedan doctors of divinity? In fact, could any one who wasn't inspired have written this?

Fear is the creator of all barbaric—all brutal—religions. It is the foundation of our Christian faith.

Says Lecky:

> "Terror is everywhere the beginning of religion. The phenomena which impress themselves most forcibly on the mind of the savage are not those which enter manifestly into the sequence of natural laws and which are productive of most beneficial effects, but those which are disastrous and apparently abnormal. Gratitude is less vivid than fear, and the smallest apparent infraction of a natural law produces a deeper impression than the most sublime of its ordinary operations. When, therefore, the most startling and terrible aspects of nature are presented to his mind, when the more deadly forms of disease or natural convulsion desolate his land, the savage derives from these things an intensely realized perception of diabolical presence. In the darkness of the night; amid the yawning chasms and the wild echoes of the mountain gorge; under the blaze of the comet, or the solemn gloom of the eclipse; when famine has blasted the land; when the earthquake and the pestilence have slaughtered their thousands; in every form of disease which refracts and distorts the reason; in all that is strange, portentous, and deadly, he feels and cowers before the supernatural. Completely exposed to all the influences of nature, and completely ignorant of the chain of sequence that unites its various parts, he lives in continued dread of what he deems the direct and isolated acts of evil spirits. Feel-

ing them continually near him, he will naturally endeavor to enter into communion with them. He will strive to propitiate them with gifts."

Thus it is that prayer, and ceremony, and sacrifice are started. And then some savage, more cunning than the rest, and realizing the power the imaginary spirits exert over the minds of his fellows, "will," says Lecky, "attempt to invest himself with their authority; and his excited imagination will soon persuade him that he has succeeded in his desire. If his abilities and his ambition place him above the common level, he will find in this belief the most ready path to power."

And so the priest evolved from the voodoo conjurer of the jungle; and Jehovah is but the image of the "wild echoes of the mountain gorge"; and Satan is the personification of "every form of disease which refracts and distorts the reason;" and Hell is the blazing tail of the comet; and the lords of earth, that live off the labor of others, are veneered savage chiefs of the younger world; and their courts and laws, that make robbery of the workers legal, are the reflex of the one-time stone clubs: and the creeds of Christendom are the nightmares of what was once "strange, portentous, and deadly."

As of old, man "feels and cowers before the supernatural."

Fear made heresy a crime—fear that an angry god would damn the believers if they allowed the heretic to live. Fear made the blue laws—it makes them still—fear that God will damn the Sabbath observers, if they do not punish the Sabbath breakers. To worship the wrong god. or to worship the right god the wrong way, is punishable by death here and Hell-fire hereafter. Satan is making sinners every minute, and Jehovah is damning them as fast as Satan makes them. Fear sees strange apparitions, believes impossibilities, and seeks help in supplications. The vilest liquor does not produce such delirium tremens as superstition does with the weak-minded. The worse the superstition, like the worse the liquor, the worse the delirium tremens. Christianity, with Mohammedanism a close second—both springing from the same inspired revelations—has loaded more snakes into human brains than any of the religions of earth. In ages gone by the vast majority were insane with the Christian creed. Many still go insane through believing it. Case after case of this kind continually occur. A man in Syracuse, New York, killed his mother in order that she might go to Heaven. He was a convert at a big revival meeting. Another revival convert, a young man, of Philadelphia, committed suicide. He also expected to reach Heaven. The Holy Virgin Ella may not be known in the religious circles of your locality, but she is apparently quite a character out in Los Angeles, California. She has, we are told, experienced an immaculate conception, and has given birth to a "blue-eyed, light-haired" child of Heaven. This seems all the more remarkable, or even miraculous, for the reason that Saint Ella is a chocolate brunette.

The supernatural affair recently came into prominence on account of court proceedings in which the holy colored virgin was the defendant. Says the *Los Angeles Times* of April 24, 1917:

> "Queen or Saint Ella Smith, head of the Church of the Invisible God, sat enthroned as a queen surrounded by her ladies in waiting, in Judge Taft's court yesterday. Saint Ella is a colored woman, past the meridian of life, whose followers are largely white men and women. White women flanked her right and left. As members of her church, they had heard of the tremendous event predicted by Saint Ella, no less than the coming of a King Emmanuel. But it remained for Etta Russell Sneath, a comely young woman and a follower of Saint Ella, to give verbal testimony to this supernatural birth.
>
> "The remarkable colored woman was in court as a defendant in the suit of Miss R. M. Bekins to recover possession of property at 962 East Thirty-third Street, upon which the church is located. Martin Bekins, the father, who owned the property, had occasionally attended the meetings formerly held at another location. Mrs. Smith had told him of her desire to acquire the Thirty-third street property.

"Mr. Bekins finally bought the land and the church was built, the condition being, according to Bekins, that Mrs. Smith could use it, rent free, as long as she continued her present teachings and services. He deeded the property to his daughter.

"He was corroborated by I. H. Preston, who had contributed a lot worth $500. But early in 1916, Mr. Bekins testified, Mrs. Smith branched off into another channel. This was to become the mother of a King Emmanuel, who was to be a spirit to guide the faithful into holiness and truth. The great event is alleged to have occurred June 3, 1916. Followers of Mrs. Smith are alleged to have told of the visions they had of this child, a blue-eyed, light-haired boy."

Isn't it wonderful?

And how easily Saint Ella convinces men and women—white ones at that—to believe her story! She doubtless uses the same logic that the learned theologians use to prove the divine birth of Christ.

There is no reason why this logic should not apply in one case as well as the other.

The evidence would fit either.

Whether or not Saint Ella's child is to be finally offered up in sacrifice" to satisfy the wrath of his ghostly begetter is not disclosed. All we know is that he is "a spirit to guide the faithful into holiness and the truth."

Doubtless the regularly ordained reverends will denounce Saint Ella as a fraud. However, outside of a natural objection to any competition in the superstition business, there is no apparent reason why they should do so. A colored lady has just as good a right as anybody to become the mother of a god, and the happening is no more to be questioned these days than it was centuries ago. Other races, Chinese, Hindoos, Japanese, etc., boast of holy virgins that were the mothers of divinely begotten sons. It would not be fair to have the darkies left out. It would be showing partiality on the part of the divine progenitors, whoever and wherever they are. Of course it requires faith to believe that a god did it, but you cannot limit faith. The minute you do it isn't faith. The more impossible anything appears, the more faith it requires to believe it. The way to acquire faith is to refuse to reason and center your mind on belief. Faith then becomes a habit, like chewing tobacco, or smoking cigarettes. The more it is practiced the tighter it sticks to you. "Faith," says an inspired authority, "is the substance of things hoped for, the evidence of things not seen." This is exactly the case of Saint Ella. A divinely conceived "King Emmanuel" was doubtless Saint Ella's "substance of things hoped for." That the thing "hoped for" came to pass is readily proven by "the evidence of things unseen."

If this isn't orthodox, what is?

It therefore ill becomes orthodox Christians to denounce the colored Saint Ella and her divinely begotten, blue-eyed, light-haired child as a fraud. Orthodox Christians offer the world too big a load of past-gone impossibilities themselves to denounce Saint Ella's present-day impossibility. They should not put themselves in the same category with the ancient Jews whom they religiously condemn for not believing the Virgin Mary story. Of course, they can hardly be expected to welcome the colored Virgin Ella and her King Emmanuel into their scheme of divinely ordained delusions, but they should bear in mind that people in glass houses shouldn't throw stones.

At best—or at worst—the acceptance of this late manifestation of the mysteries of religion would but add one more saint and one more god to the already recognized saints and deities. The canonization of the colored Ella into a saint couldn't possibly bring much more affliction to the Christian world than we already have. And the recognizing of a holy quartet instead of a holy trinity would only require the building of one more gold throne in the skies. Considering what they have accomplished already, it certainly would not put much of a strain on the brains of the theologians to announce an addition to the god family, even if one of them was part Ethiopian.

The *St. Louis Republic*, in its issue of May 21, 1917, published the following press dispatch, from Kansas City, Missouri:

"Jacob Bentz, 35, went mad and applied the story of the Biblical sacrifice in his home early last night, when he dragged Helena, 6 years old, his oldest child, into a room and beat her to death with a sewing machine.

"Two hours later Bentz was found with his Bible opened at the passage from Genesis XXII, 1, kneeling beside his dead child, his hands clasped in prayer. He did not resist arrest, and murmured:

"'It was God's will that I killed my child,' as he was taken to jail. In the other room Mrs. Bentz lay prostrated, clutching her three remaining children.

"Bentz has been employed at the Swift packinghouse since coming to Kansas City several years ago. He was known to be deeply religious, and read his Bible at every opportunity. He wandered away from home three nights ago, and was found asleep the next morning in the East Bottoms, five miles away.

"The sacrifice of his daughter was premeditated. Abraham, of Biblical times, went on a three days' journey before offering Isaac to the Lord. Bentz quit work at the packing-house three days ago. Early last night Bentz took out his Bible and turned to his favorite theme. Suddenly he closed the book and taking Helena by the hand, forced her to leave her mother and enter another room with him. The mother attempted to follow, but he pushed her back and locked the door.

"'Isaac's life was saved by God. Did you expect God to spare your child?' Bentz was asked in his cell.

"'God told me to sacrifice her,' was all he would say."

Only a short time previous to the foregoing exhibition of religious madness a notorious revivalist had held forth for several weeks in Kansas City.

Is it possible that any considerable portion of the people of this country could again be driven back to the dark days when the Bible was believed from cover to cover by the majority of men and women?

Will were-wolves again be seen by holy men, and Satan's witches burned at the stake?

In "A Fool's Commentary of Scripture and Doctrine," a recently published little book of exquisite satire, by "Pater Guilielmus," we read that "war is something which originated among the angels in Heaven,—which shows that you can never tell when and where it may break out." Can men that can be led forth to shoot each other, by powers that claim to be following Jehovah, be led to torture and burn again those whom these powers might charge with being servants of Satan?

The lesson is plain: Society is not safe so long as it acknowledges the power of any class to rule either the body or brain. A ruling class government is as much of a myth as religion. If the workers of the world were wise they would submit to neither. They would obliterate all national boundary lines, and dwell upon the earth in "Life, Liberty, and the pursuit of Happiness."

9. Satan's Sorceries in New England

From the war-madness of the twentieth century, let us go back to the witchcraft madness of the seventeenth. Let us go back to Calvinism's New Jerusalem, the town of Salem, Massachusetts.

Says Bancroft (*History of the United States*):

"New England, like Canaan, had been settled by fugitives. Like the Jews, they had fled to a wilderness; like the Jews, they looked to Heaven for light to lead them on; like the Jews, they had no supreme ruler but God; like the Jews, they had heathen for their foes; and they derived their legislation from the Jewish code. But for the people of New England, the days of Moses and Joshua were passed; for them there was no longer a promised land—they were in possession. Reason now insisted on bringing the adopted laws to the proof, that it might hold fast only to the good.

The writer fails to see 'reason' here at work. The word to describe it is superstition.

"Skepticism began to appear. The fear of sorcery and the Evil Power of the invisible world had sprung alike from the letter of the Mosaic law and from the wonder excited by the mysteries of nature. The belief in witchcraft had fastened itself on the elements of faith and become deeply branded into the common mind. * * * In the settlement of New England, the temple, or, as it was called, the meeting house, was the center round which the people gathered. As the Church had successfully assumed the exclusive possession of civil franchises, the ambition of the ministers had been both excited and gratified. They were not only the counselors by an unwritten law, they were the authors of state papers, often employed on embassies, and, at home, speakers at elections and in town meetings."

There never were more fervent believers in the Bible than the Puritans. They followed Jehovah's every command. Their religion may be summed up as worshiping God, dreading Satan, and hating mankind. They made a holy covenant, which read: "We covenant with the Lord, and one with another, and do bind ourselves in the presence of God, to walk together in all His ways, according as He is pleased to reveal Himself to us, in His blessed word of truth."

In order to faithfully follow that "blessed word of truth" the Puritans selected the loudest-mouthed lunatics to be found and made ministers of them; and these ministers, in turn, dictated as to who should be governors and legislators, judges and juries, justices of the peace and constables, jailers and hangmen, and all other civil officials.

Jehovah of the jungle reigned supreme.

In Massachusetts no man could be governor unless he was a professing Christian, worth at least $5,000. And the Puritan ministers dictated as to the sort of Christianity he should profess. Governors Endicott and Winthrop were shining examples of these Christian officials. All they knew was what they learned from the Bible. That they knew the Bible, believed it and followed it, is evidenced in the history of the period. "Endicott and Winthrop had both signed death warrants for persons convicted of the crime (witchcraft); or at least had not stayed the executions of the condemned."[i]

Says this same writer:

"Between the settlement of Salem by Roger Conant in 1626 and the witchcraft days of 1692, the intolerance of the Puritans had been strikingly manifested on more than one occasion. The Brownes had been sent back to England for differing from Endicott and the First Church people; Endicott had cut the red cross from the flag because it reminded him of popery; Roger Williams had been banished from the colony for preaching that men should be allowed freedom of conscience in religious matters; Quakers had been hung in Boston, and Quaker women, half naked, dragged through the streets of Salem at the tail of a cart and whipped, for maintaining the doctrines of their sect. All this by a people who, within half a century, had come to these shores to worship according to the dictates of conscience. So, also, Thomas Scrugg, a deputy and a judge of the local court, for sympathy with Ann Hutchinson's Antimonian views, was proscribed, disarmed and deprived of his public functions; William Alford, for sympathizing with Scrugg, was censured and disarmed and left the colony; Richard Waterman, an intelligent, industrious man and law-abiding citizen, for dissenting from the severe policy of the leading men of the colony, was imprisoned and banished; even Townsend Bishop, in 1645, because he did not promptly bring forward an infant for baptism, was handed over for discipline, and he a deputy and local magistrate. Lady Deborah Moody, because she doubted the necessity of infant baptism, was compelled to leave the colony. Even in a much later day, William Gray was persecuted in Salem for opinion's sake, and driven from the city."

---

i   Winfield S. Nevins, "Witchcraft in Salem Village"

The following graphic description is given of the whipping of Quakers:

"Peter Pearson and Judith Brown, being stripped to the waist, were fastened to a cart-tail and whipped through the town of Boston. Joseph Southick also was stripped and led through the streets of Boston at the cart-tail and vehemently scourged by the hangman. The same day he was whipped at Roxbury, and the next morning at Dedham. The whip used for these executions was not of whip-cord, but of dried guts, and each string had three knots at the end. At Dover, Anne Coleman, Mary Tomkins, and Alice Ambrose were sentenced to be fastened to the cart-tail and whipped on their naked backs through eleven towns, a distance of nearly eighty miles. Then, on a very cold day, the deputy, Walden, at Dover, caused these women to be stripped naked, from the middle upward, and tied to a cart, and then whipped them, while the preacher looked on and laughed at it. Two of their friends testified against Walden's cruelty, for which they were put in the stocks. The women were carried to Hampton, and there whipped; from thence to Salisbury, and again whipped. William Barefoot at length obtained the warrant from the constable for their release, the preacher, however, protesting. Not long after, these women returned to Dover, and were again seized, while in meeting, and barbarously dragged about at the instigation of Hateevil Nutwell, a ruling elder. * * * They were dragged by their arms nearly a mile through a deep snow, across fields and over stumps, by which they were much bruised. The next day they were dragged down a steep hill to the water side and threatened with drowning, and one of them was actually plunged into the water, when a sudden shower obliged the Christians to retreat. At length, after much abuse, these victims of orthodox barbarity were turned out of doors at midnight; and, with their clothes wet and frozen, were obliged to suffer the inclemency of a severe winter's night. Afterward Anne Coleman and four of her friends were whipped through Salem, Boston, and Dedham by order of Hawthorne, the magistrate. Anne Coleman was a little weakly woman, and, while she was fastened to the cart at Dedham, the executioner, encouraged by the Puritan minister Bellingman, struck her so savagely that, with the knot of the whip, he split the nipple of her breast, which so tortured her that it almost took away her life."[i]

Margaret Brewster was the last Quaker woman whipped. She had gone to New England to protest to the governor against his cruel course. She was tried and condemned, her sentence being in the following words: "Margaret" Brewster, You are to have your clothes stripped off to the middle, and to be tied to a cart's tail at the South Meeting House, and to be drawn through the town, and to receive twenty stripes upon your naked body."

Says Brooks Adams, in his "Emancipation of Massachusetts":

"Viewed from the standpoint of comparative history, the policy of theocratic Massachusetts toward the Quakers was the necessary consequence of antecedent causes, and is exactly paralleled with the massacre of the house of Ahab by Elisha and Jehu (as told in 2 Kings ix, x). The power of a dominant priesthood depended on conformity, and the Quakers absolutely refused to conform; nor was this the blackest of their crimes; they believed that the deity communicated directly with men, and that these revelations were the highest rules of conduct. Manifestly such a doctrine was revolutionary. The influence of all ecclesiastics must ultimately rest upon the popular belief that they are endowed with attributes which are denied to common men. The

---

[i] Macdonald's "History of the Inquisition," quoted from "Champions of the Church."

syllogism of the New England elders was this: All revelation was contained in the Bible; we alone, from our peculiar education, are capable of interpreting the meaning of the scriptures; therefore we only can declare the will of God. But it. is evident that, were the dogma of the 'inner light' once accepted, this reasoning must fall to the ground, and the authority of the ministry be overthrown. Necessarily those who held so subversive a doctrine would be pursued with greater hate than less harmful heretics, and thus contemplating the situation there is no difficulty in understanding why the Rev. John Wilson, pastor, Boston, should have vociferated in his pulpit, that 'he would carry fire in one hand and faggots in the other, to burn all the Quaker--; in the world;' why the Rev. John Higginson should haw. denounced the 'inner light' as 'a stinking vapour from Hell;' why the astute Norton should have taught that the 'justice of God was the Devil's armour;' and why Endicott sternly warned the first comers, 'Take heed you break not our ecclesiastical laws, for then ye are sure to stretch by the halter.'"

So absolutely was New England in the hands of Jehovah that a heathen Indian chief[i] remarked, "What a God have the English, who deal so with one another about their God!"

We read that in the year 1657 "Anne Burden and Mary Dyer were imprisoned at Boston; and Mary Clark, for warning these persecutors to desist from their iniquity, was unmercifully rewarded with twenty stripes of a three-corded whip on her naked back, and detained in prison about three months in the winter season. The cords of these whips were commonly as thick as a man's little finger, each cord having knots at the end. Christopher Holder and John Copeland were whipped at Boston the same year, each thirty stripes with a knotted whip of three cords, the hangman measuring his ground and fetching the strokes with all the force he could, 'which

---

i   Cotton Mather denounced the Indians as the offspring of Satan.

Satan's Sorceries in New England

so cruelly cut their flesh that a woman standing by fell down dead.' Then they were locked up in prison and kept three days without food, or so much as a drink of water, and detained in prison nine weeks in the cold winter season, without fire, bed, or straw. They afterwards had their right ears cut off by authority. Lawrence and Cassandra Southick and their son Josiah, being carried to Boston, were all of them, notwithstanding the old age of the two, sent to the house of correction, and whipped with cords as those before, in the coldest season of the year."[i]

Nor were the Puritanical "Blue Laws" confined to New England. They existed, under the domination of the Episcopal Church, as well as under the Presbyterian. To a somewhat lesser extent they exist in various parts of this country to this day. Thomas Jefferson, in his "Notes on Virginia," writes: "The first settlers [of Virginia] were emigrants from England, of the English church, just at a point of time when it was flushed with complete victory over the religions of all other persuasions. Possessed as they became of the powers of making, administering, and executing the laws, they showed equal intolerance in this country with their Presbyterian brethren who had emigrated to the Northern government. * * * Several acts of the Virginia Assembly, of 1659, 1662, and 1693 had made it penal in parents to refuse to have their children baptized; had prohibited the 'unlawful' assembling of Quakers; had made it penal for any master of a vessel to bring a Quaker into the state; had ordered those already there, and such as should come thereafter, to be imprisoned till they should abjure the country—provided a milder penalty for the first and second return, but death for their third. If no capital executions took place here, as did in New England, it was not owing to the moderation of the Church, or spirit of the legislature, as may be inferred from the law itself; but to historical circumstances which have not been handed down to us."

---

[i] Macdonald's "History of the Inquisition," quoted from "Champions of the Church"

Trusting that the reader will find considerable amusement, as well as being furnished with a historical warning against all Puritanical and sumptuary legislation against Satan's alleged sorceries, scandals and temptations, realizing where unchecked religious and prohibitive bigotry, as disclosed in all laws against personal liberty, at last leads to, the following, taken from the Biblical laws of the Puritans, as compiled in the "Blue Laws of Connecticut" (Truth Seeker Co., N. Y.), gathered from the public records of the period, are presented:

If any man after legal conviction, shall have or worship any other God but the Lord God, he shall bee put to death.—Deut. 13. 6—17. 2.—Exodus 22. 20.

If any man or woman be a Witch, that is, hath or consulteth with a familiar spirit, they shall be put to death.—Exo. 22. 18.—Levit. 20. 27.—Deut. 18. 10, 11.

If any person shall blaspheme the name of God the father, Son or holy Ghost, with direct, express, presumptuous or highhanded blasphemy, or shall curse in the like manner, he shall be put too death.— Lev. 24. 15, 16.

If any person shall commit any willful murder, which is manslaughter committed upon malice, hatred or cruelty, not in a man's necessary and just defense, nor by mere casualty against his will, he shall be put to death.—Exo. 21. 12, 13, 14.—Numb. 35. 30, 31.

If any person shall slay another through guile, either by poisonings or other such Devilish practice, he shall be put to death.—Exo. 21. 14.

If any person committeth adultery with a married or espoused wife, the Adulterer and the Adulteress shall surely be put to death.— Levit. 20. 10, and 18.20.— Deut. 22. 23, 24.

If any man shall forcibly, and without consent, Ravish any maide, or woman that is lawfully married or contracted, he shall be put to death.—Deut. 22. 25.[i]

If any man stealeth a man or mankind, he shall be put to death.—Exodus 21. 16.

If any man rise up by false witness, wittingly and of purpose to take away any man's life, he shall be put to death.—Deut. 19, 16. 18. 19.

If any man shall conspire or attempt any invasion, insurrection or rebellion against the Commonwealth, he shall be put to death.

If any Childe or Children above sixteen years old and of sufficient understanding, shall Curse or smite their natural father or mother, he or they shall be put to death; unless it can be sufficiently testified that the parents have been very unchristianly negligent in the education of such children, or so provoke them by extreme or cruel correction that they have been forced thereunto to preserve themselves from death or maiming.—Exo. 21.17.— Levit. 20.—Ex. 21. 15.

If any man have a stubborn and rebellious son of sufficient years and understanding, viz. Sixteen years 'of age, which shall not obey the voice of his father or the voice of his mother, and that when they have chastened him will not hearken unto them; then may his father and mother, being his natural parents, lay hold on him and bring him to the Magistrates assembled in Court, and testify unto them, that their son is stubborn and rebellious and will not obey their voice and Chastisement, but lives in sundry notorious Crimes, such a son shall be put to death.—Deut. 21. 20, 21.

---

i   The reader will note that this law did not apply to an unmarried woman, or one not engaged to be married. The Puritans strictly followed the Biblical law that made a married or betrothed woman the personal property of the man.

Forasmuch, as the open contempt of God's word, and messengers thereof, is the desolating sin of civil states and churches, and that the preaching of the word by those whom God doth send, is the chief ordinary means ordained by God, for the converting, edifying and saving the souls of the elect, through the presence and power of the Holy Ghost thereunto promised; and that the ministry of the word is set up by God in his churches for those holy ends; and according to the respect of contempt of the same, and of those whom God hath set apart for his own work and employment, the weale or woe of all Christian states, is much furthered and promoted:

It is therefore ordered and decreed, That if any Christian, so called, within this jurisdiction, shall contemptuously bear himself towards the word preached, or the messengers that are called to dispense the same in any congregation, when he doth faithfully execute his service and office therein, according to the will and word of God, either by interrupting him in his preaching, or by charging him falsely with an error, which he hath not taught in the open face of the church, or like a son of Korah, cast upon his true doctrine, or himself, any reproach to the dishonor of the Lord Jesus, who hath sent him-and to the disparagement of that his holy ordinance, and making Gods ways contemptible and ridiculous, that every such person or persons, whatsoever censure the church may pass, shall, for the first scandal, be convented and reproved openly, by the magistrates, at some lecture, and bound to their good behavior: And if a second time they break forth into the like contemptuous carriages, they shall either pay five pounds to the public treasure, or stand two hours openly, upon a block or stool four foot high, upon a lecture day, with a paper fixed on his breast written with capital letters, AN OPEN AND OBSTINATE CONTEMNER OF GODS HOLY ORDINANCES, that others may fear and be ashamed of breaking out into the like wickedness.

It is ordered and decreed by this court and authority thereof, That wheresoever the ministry of the word is established, according to the order of the gospel, throughout this jurisdiction, every person shall duly resort and attend thereunto respectively, upon the Lord's day, and upon such public fast days, and day of thanksgiving, as are to be generally kept by the appointment of authority: And if any person within this jurisdiction shall, without just and necessary cause, withdraw himself from hearing the public ministry of the word, after due means of conviction used, he shall forfeit for his absence, from every such public meeting, five shillings: All such offences to bee heard and determined by any one magistrate, or more, from time to time.

The following law regarding servants, is in strict accord with the teachings of St. Paul:

It is also ordered by the authority aforesaid, That no servant, either man or maid, shall either give, sell or truck, any commodity whatsoever, without license from their master, during the time of their service, under pain of fine or corporal punishment, at the discretion of the Court, as the offence shall deserve; and that all workmen shall work the whole day, allowing convenient time for food and rest.

It is also ordered, That when any servants shall run from their masters, or any other inhabitants shall privately go away with suspicion of ill intentions, it shall bee lawful for the next magistrate, or the constable and two of the chiefest inhabitants, where no magistrate is, to press men and boats or pinnaces, at the public charge, to pursue such persons by sea or land, and bring them back, by force of arms.

And here is a law that present day Puritans, in some localities, are re-enacting:

It is ordered by the authority of this Court, That no person under the age of twenty one years, nor any other, that hath not already accustomed himself to the use thereof, shall take any tobacco, until he hath brought a certificate under the hands of some who are approved for knowledge and skill in physic, that it is useful for him, and also, that he hath received a license from the court for the same.—And for the regulating of those, who either by their former taking it, have, to their own apprehensions, made it necessary to them, or upon due advice, are persuaded to the use thereof.

It is ordered, That no man within this colony, after the publication hereof, shall take any tobacco publicly, in the street, highways or any barn yards, or upon training days, in any open places, under the penalty of six-pence for each offence against this order, in any the particulars thereof, to bee paid without gainsaying, upon conviction, by the testimony of one witness, that is without just exception, before any one magistrate. And the constables in the several towns, are required to make presentment to each particular court, of such as they doe understand, and can evict to be transgressors of this order.

A copy of the warrant is preserved under which the three Quaker women, Anne Coleman, Mary Tomkins, and Alice Ambrose were tied to the tail of a cart and publicly whipped. It runs as follows:

"To the Constables of Dover, Hampton, Salisbury, New-bury, Rowley, Ipswich, Wenham, Linn, Boston, Roxbury, Dedham, and until these vagabond Quakers are carried out of this jurisdiction.

"You and every one of you are required, in the King's Majesty's name, to take these vagabond Quakers, Anne Coleman, Mary Tomkins, and Alice Ambrose, and make them fast to the cart's tail, and driving the cart through your several towns, to whip them on their backs, not exceeding ten stripes apiece on each of them in each town, and so to convey them from constable to constable, till they come out of this jurisdiction, and you will answer it at your peril: and this shall be your warrant.

"Per me, RICHARD WALDEN.

"At Dover, dated December 22d, 1662."

Alas! for the crimes that are committed in the name of God and Devil. The worship demanded by the one, and the fright inspired by the other, have filled the world with cruelty. In his efforts to obtain Heaven and escape Hell man has been made a brute. He is a victim of the horrors; his brain is diseased with religious delirium tremens. He is a peripatetic marionette worked by an hypnotic power. Put a gold crown on a worthless creature, anoint him in the name of God, and the human marionettes are on their knees. Adorn a dunce with a holy title—call him a reverend—and he will tell of gods and goblins, heavens and hells, and the human marionettes shake in their boots. Let a brass band break loose with "God Save the King," or Kaiser, or Bethlehem Steel, and the marionettes hop to their feet and howl themselves hoarse. Shake a strip of silk or muslin decorated with lions, or eagles, or symbols of some sort, in their faces, and they go as batty as a barnyard bull at the sight of a red flannel shirt. They will follow it into the very jaws of death. All they ask is that the reverend promises that his goblins won't get them after they are gone. Man will let a creature of his own breed write some "herein-be-it-knowns" on a sheet of paper and take possession of the earth. The landless and homeless will then pay tribute to the sheet of paper in order to stay here. After being buncoed out of everything that Mother Nature gave him, man passes laws that locks him up in jails, that he builds himself, if he takes, in order to satisfy his wants, any of the products, which he himself has produced by his labor, that the sheet of paper says belongs to the creature that lives without work. Under the spell of royalty, reverends, and robbers, man endures an existence that no other animals would stand for.

Come out of it, open your eyes and behold! The beautiful, bounteous Earth is our only country, the life-giving Sun the only overlord! The boundless canopy of blue that bends above us the only temple dome, the Spirit of Nature the only god!

Come out of it, and be free and happy, be lovers and comrades, and not haters and cutthroats for lordly loafers that live by the ravishment of you, and your wives and your children.

10. Massachusetts Under the Rein of the Doctors of Delusion

With the exception of John Calvin, Protestantism never produced a more raving maniac than Cotton Mather. He went through life with Satan at his heels. He said, "No place, that I know of, has got such a spell upon it as will always keep the Devil out. * * * Only when we come to Heaven, we shall be out of his reach forever."

He wrote a book on the "Wonders of the Invisible World." One of these wonders was the sight of countless unbaptized infants, less than a span long, burning in Hell. His god even damned miscarriages. Another was the happiness expressed on the faces of the saved as they leaned over the jasper walls of Heaven and viewed the agony of the lost in Hell. Religion had driven from his soul every spark of humanity, had driven from his brain every particle of reason. He was dead-drunk with divinity dope—a hopeless victim of the holy horrors. It was nothing for him to see an old woman astride a broomstick riding over the moon. Cotton Mather thundered his delusions from the pulpit, and the masses believed them. They, too, became victims of the holy horrors. They became as mad as those that shriek for war.

Then started in New England a witchcraft craze that forms one of the most brutal chapters in church history. The first victim of the inspired insanity, "Thou shalt not suffer a witch to live," was a woman named Margaret Jones. Her trial, sufferings and death, were enough, it would seem, to make it a crime to proclaim that a book containing that savage injunction is the Word of God. The evidence that condemned her as a witch is preserved in the journals of John Winthrop, governor of the colony at the time, and who presided at the trial. He says that "she was found to have such a malignant touch as many persons, men, women and children, whom she stroked or touched with any affection or displeasure were taken with deafness, or vomiting, or other violent pains or sickness." Gov. Winthrop further declares that "in the prison there was seen in her arms a little child which ran from her into another room and the officer following it, it vanished".[i] That Gov. Winthrop's brain was diseased with religious superstition is shown in his declaration that the "same day and hour she was executed, there was a very great tempest at Connecticut which blew down many trees."

Jehovah was trying to blow Satan out of New England, like he once forced him over the ramparts of Heaven.

Winfield S. Nevins (Witchcraft in Salem Village) quotes the story found in "Everett's Anecdotes of Early Local History":

> "Shortly after the execution of Margaret Jones, her husband endeavored to secure passage to Barbados in a vessel then lying in Boston harbor with a hundred and eighty tons of ballast and eighty horses on board. He was refused passage because he was the husband of a witch, and 'it was immediately observed that the vessel began to roll as if it would turn over.' This strange action was alleged to be caused by Jones. The magistrates, being notified, issued their warrants for his arrest. As the officer, going to serve the warrant, was crossing the ferry, the vessel continued to roll. He remarked that he had that which would tame the vessel and keep it quiet, at the same time exhibiting the document.

---

i quotation from Winthrop's journal in "Witchcraft in Salem Village".

Instantly the vessel ceased to roll, after having been in motion twelve hours. Jones was arrested and thrown into prison, and the vessel rolled no more."

Jehovah quit agitating the waters of Boston harbor as soon as the widower of an executed witch was securely locked up.

The reader will note the similarity of the Jones story, as recorded in the history of the New England Puritans, and the Jonah story, as recorded in the inspired word of God. If the authorities had allowed Jones to have sailed for Barbados, who knows but what Jehovah might have inspired the sailors to dump him overboard in Boston bay, where he had prepared a big codfish to swallow him? As it was, Jones finally escaped with his life. The judge and the preachers hunted the Scriptures in vain to find a passage that commanded the death of the widower of a witch. Whether Jehovah had purposely left out such an injunction, or whether he had overlooked the matter, or whether, in ancient times, witches did not marry, the doctors of divinity could not decide. The best they could do was to set aside a day of prayer. The General Court, we are told, "appointed a day of humiliation", to ask Jehovah's mercy on account "of the extent to which Satan prevails amongst us in respect of witchcraft." Within recent times we had something of the same sort—a day of prayer to keep us out of war.

Among the Puritans the male servants of Satan usually fared better than the female, except in the case of Quakers. These they hanged regardless of sex. Jehovah's injunctions, regarding those that worshiped the wrong god, or worshiped the right god the wrong way, were very explicit.

The next recorded case of witch hanging was that of Ann Hibbins, a widow living in Boston.[i]

---

[i] There were doubtless many witches hanged in those days of which no record was kept.

Her husband, at one time, was quite well off, but had met with financial reverses, and was penniless when he died. His death, together with poverty, said the neighbors, made the widow "crabbed and meddlesome." She probably had to take in washing. She became rebellious against the afflictions that God had sent upon her in order to try her faith. Well-to-do Christians always see things in this light. Finally the church censured her for complaining of her lot. As that did not appear to do her any good, in the latter part of 1655 she was accused of being a witch.

Was it not evident that Satan had gotten control of her, else why should she rebel against the poverty and misery that Jehovah had sent upon her?

Does not Jehovah choose who shall be masters, and who shall be servants?

And does he not command that servants shall be obedient and servile to their masters?

And was not Ann Hibbins to be reckoned in the servant class, now that Jehovah had taken away her husband in a bankrupt condition?

And does not St. Paul say that rebellious subjects shall be eternally damned?

Therefore was it not only the duty, but also the privilege, for God's anointed to hurry Ann Hibbins to Hell as quickly as possible? So this poor widow, as commanded by the Holy Bible, was dragged into a court composed entirely of orthodox Christians, and was found guilty of being on familiar terms with Satan. Satan would doubtless have saved her life, if he had been able, but there were too many Christians; therefore the Governor of Massachusetts said his prayers, pronounced the sentence, and Ann Hibbins was religiously hanged.

A remarkable case is that of a Mrs. Greensmith, who confessed that she had committed adultery with Satan. As she was unquestionably weak-minded, and as her husband was a Puritan, it seems to look like a case of mistaken identity.

In 1671 Elizabeth Knapp, of Groton, Massachusetts, was convicted of witchcraft. She was a hopeless lunatic; and, as all lunatics, according to the Bible, are possessed of the Devil, or even, at times, of legions of little devils, as was the case of the man from whom the alleged son of Jehovah extracted such a vast amount and sent them into a herd of swine, there was no doubt of Elizabeth Knapp's guilt; and as there was no son of Jehovah in Massachusetts to relieve her of her devils, the Puritans did as they pleased with her.

The account of the case, as told by Rev. Samuel Willard, recorded in Putnam's "Witchcraft Explained," leaves no doubt as to Elizabeth Knapp's mental condition. What caused her affliction is, of course, unknown; but this we do know, that there was enough orthodox Christianity at the time to turn her head. At most, she was no crazier than Cotton Mather, or Gov. Endicott, or even many in governmental and church authority today; and those in turn are no crazier than the people who place them there.

The history of Christendom is largely that of crafty lunatics devouring the duller ones.

Regarding the case of Elizabeth Knapp, as testified by the Rev. Willard, we read: "Elizabeth was at first subject to mental moods and violent physical actions. Strange, sudden shrieks, strange changes of countenance appeared; followed by the exclamations 'O my leg,' which she would rub; 'O my breast,' and she would rub that. Afterwards came fits in which she would cry out, 'money, money,' offered her as inducements to yield obedience, and sometimes, 'sin and misery,' as threats of punishment for refusal to obey the wishes of her strange visitant. Subsequently she barked like a dog and bleated like a calf. Then she told Mr. Willard that he was a rogue. Some voice said to her, 'I am not Satan, I am a pretty black boy, you are my pretty girl.' She charged Willard himself and some others of his parish with being her tormentors".[i]

---

[i] From this it would seem that, at times, she might have been quite sane.

It seems, according to Puritan testimony, that Satan at one time tried to make Roman Catholics of them. Whether this was to make them better, or worse than they were, is hard for an impartial student of church history to determine. It does not seem possible, however, to have made them any worse. Anyway we are told that a Mrs. Glover, who was convicted and hung as a witch in 1688, was not only a Catholic, but also a "wild Irish woman of bad character." Everybody, in the eyes of the Puritans, were wild except themselves. This Mrs. Glover worked for a Puritan family that lived in Boston, by the name of Goodwin. The Goodwins had a number of children, who, having been taught from infancy the Puritan faith, were, naturally, somewhat mentally unbalanced. We are told that Mrs. Glover "talked harshly, perhaps profanely, to the children." This threw one of them, named Martha, into fits. The other children soon followed Martha's example, and they, too, had fits. From Calvinism to fits isn't very far to go. Satan, working his spell through the Irish Catholic woman, Mrs. Glover, soon had the Goodwin youngsters fixed so that they would go into spasms at the sight of the " 'Assembly's Catechism,' Cotton Mather's 'Milk for Babes,' and some other good books." This, however, hardly seems strange. The writer, himself, when a child, nearly underwent the same experience, from being compelled to study Calvinist literature of this sort, and there was no Irish Catholic on the job. From having spasms over the Presbyterian Catechism and Cotton Mather's "Milk for Babes," the Goodwin children began to have attacks of appearing deaf, or dumb, or blind, and "sometimes all these disorders together would come upon them." They soon exhibited other evidences of Satan's sorceries—"their tongues would be drawn down their throats, then pulled out upon their chins" whenever the gospel of infant damnation was preached in their ears. On the other hand we are told that they "could read Popish and Quaker books without any difficulties." This was evidence enough against the "wild Irish woman of bad character." She was one of Satan's witches, whom the just and merciful Jehovah had condemned to death.

Massachusetts Under the Rein of the Doctors of Delusion

In the year 1692 the Rev. Samuel Parrish was pastor of the church in Salem Village. Being a follower of the Bible god, he believed in witchcraft, and was also a slave-owner. Also, like Cotton Mather, and some doctors of divinity still among us, he preached the doctrine of eternal torment.

He was an orthodox Christian in every sense of the word.

Before coming to Massachusetts the Rev. Samuel Parrish had lived in the West Indies, where he had preached the glad tidings of Calvinism to the natives.

Among his household chattels, that he had brought with him to Salem Village, was a female slave, half negro and half native West Indian, named Tituba. At that time the Christians, following the divinely ordained law regarding slaves, as found in the twenty-fifth chapter of Leviticus, verse 44, "Both thy bondmen, and thy bondmaids, which thou shalt have, shall be of the heathen that are round about you," were, whenever possible, enslaving the Indians. America to them was the Promised Land, that Jehovah had furnished with every good thing, among which was a large supply of heathen ready to be seized as slaves.

But Satan had got hold of the Indians and had filled their hearts with rebellion against Jehovah's laws. In fact, as before mentioned, Cotton Mather finally decided that the Indians were all devils, the natural children of Satan himself. He had sufficient reason, from an orthodox standpoint, to think so. Negro slaves were made contented with their lot with hallelujah hymns of the sweet by and by, but the Indians did not seem to appreciate the beauties of the white man's religion. And so it happened quite frequently that when a husky young heathen Indian was captured, and the Bible law regarding slavery was read to him, that, instead of inspiring him with servility, it filled his devilish nature with revenge; and, instead of arising at sun-up to hoe corn for his Christian master, he stealthily arose in the middle of the night, went to the woodpile and armed himself with an ax, found his way to his master's bedside, and hurried the pious creature to Heaven before he had any idea of going there. Satan's offspring would then, without bothering to consult any divinely inspired book, appropriate the best horse on the place, and light put for his native wilds. This naturally had a tendency to discourage Indian slavery.

But to return to the Rev. Samuel Parrish and his bondmaid Tituba. It was in the home of this Puritan preacher that witchcraft was fanned into a raging fury in Salem Village; and the half-negro slave woman, Tituba, together with Elizabeth, the nine-year-old daughter of Parris, and a niece who lived with him, Abigail Williams, eleven years of age, together with other children of the neighborhood, were, we are told, the ones that started it. It is said that during the winter "these girls held occasional meetings in the nighborhood, usually at the minister's house. * * * They began to act after a strange and unusual manner, by getting into holes and creeping under chairs and stools, and to use sundry odd postures and antic gestures, uttering foolish, ridiculous speeches, which neither they themselves nor any others could make any sense of."[i]

We further read:

> "This state of affairs continuing from late in December until into February, 1692, the elder people learned something of what was transpiring in their midst. Great was their consternation. Dr. Griggs was called, but, as sometimes happens, even in this age of great learning, the doctor did not know what ailed the young people. Their 'disease' was one unknown to medical science. Evidently feeling obliged to give some explanation of the disorder, the doctor declared the girls were possessed of the Devil, in other words bewitched. Thereupon the curiosity of the whole community was awakened. People came from far and near to witness the strange antics of these children. Their credulity was taxed to its utmost. Mr. Parris, as was natural, was not only an interested spectator, but he took charge of the whole business. He called

---

i   Winfield S. Nevins, *Witchcraft in Salem Village*

a meeting of the ministers of the neighboring parishes to observe, to investigate, to pray. They came; they saw; they were conquered."[i]

Satan was now working overtime with his sorceries in Salem Village. Recognizing in the Puritans a people after Jehovah's own heart, he proposed to do his utmost to destroy their religion. His aim was to eventually make a witch or a wizard out of every male and female Puritan. That would put an end to Puritanism and swell the population of Hell.

Finally, we are told, the preachers "unanimously agreed with Dr. Griggs that the girls were bewitched. The all-important question was, Who or what caused them to act as they did? Who bewitched them? Whose spirit did the Devil take to afflict them? Mr. Parrish and some of the ministers and prominent people of the village undertook to solve the mystery. Several private fasts were held at the minister's house, and several more were held publicly. The children at first refused to tell anything about the mysterious affair. Tituba professed to know how to discover witches, and tried some experiments with that end in view. With the assistance of her husband (also a slave belonging to Rev. Parrish) she mixed some meal with urine of the afflicted and made a cake."[ii]

No sooner had Tituba fed the cake to the children than they knew who the parties were that bewitched them. They became as wise as Ezekiel, who, we are told, fed on a somewhat similar diet. The children charged two old women of the village, together with Tituba, as having bewitched them. The names of these two women were Sarah Good and Sarah Osburn. The history of the period describes Sarah Good as "a melancholy, distracted person," and Sarah Osburn as "a bed-ridden old woman." It was no trouble at all for the Christians to convict such creatures as these. Sarah Good was convicted of being a witch of Satan, and was hanged on July 19, 1692.

---

i   Winfield S. Nevins, *Witchcraft in Salem Village*
ii   *Ibid.*

A prominent Puritan preacher, the Rev. Noyes, was present at the hanging, and said to the victim as she stood on the scaffold: "You are a witch, and you know you are a witch." "You are a liar," was Sarah Good's indignant reply; "I am no more a witch than you are a wizard, and if you take my life, God will give you blood to drink."

Sarah Osburn was dragged from her sick bed by the faithful followers of Jehovah, and thrown into jail. It was too much for her old, wornout body, and she died before Jehovah's saints could carry out their god's command.

Whether Jehovah tried to keep her alive until she could be religiously executed, and failed, or whether Satan himself put the finishing touch on her, is. a question that only the theologians can settle.

Tituba, as well as the other women, denied being a witch, and was put in jail. Economic determinism, however, saved Tituba's life. She was never tried. She was a slave and still comparatively young, and worth good money. This, in the eyes of the Christians, is even more important than their religion. There were witness fees, and other incidentals to be paid, so Tituba was sold by the court to the highest bidder, and the money pocketed by the holy men of God.

Then began a wholesale rounding up of witches that filled the jails. Gov. Phips, then Governor of Massachusetts, coming to Boston "found the jails filled with persons accused of witchcraft." He immediately appointed a court of Oyer and Terminer to try them. William Stoughton, Deputy Governor, presided as chief justice. Having been educated for the ministry, there can be no question regarding Justice Stoughton's fitness as a judge in witch trials. Preliminary examinations were held in the churches, at which, of course, Jehovah and Satan were both present. Jehovah, with the help of the Puritans, generally won the case, and the witch was hung.

How many were put to death, and in what localities, we do not know. Gallows Hill, between Salem and Peabody, claims most of the hangings. A letter written in Salem, dated November 25, 1791, by the Rev. Dr. Hoi-yoke, contains the following information:

Massachusetts Under the Rein of the Doctors of Delusion

> "In the last month there died a man in this town, by the name of John Symonds, aged a hundred years lacking about six months, having been born in the famous '92. He has told me that his nurse had often told him, that while she was attending his mother at the time she lay in with him, she saw from the chamber windows, those unhappy people hanging on Gallows Hill, who were executed for witches by the delusion of the times."

The court of Oyer and Terminer, appointed by Gov. Phips, sat for the first time in Salem in June, 1692. There are no complete records of the court to be found. Perhaps they were so busy convicting and hanging witches that only a few cases were recorded. We do not know. We only know that at that time Jehovah's saints were having a lively time with Satan's sorceries. Gov. Hutchinson, in his History of Massachusetts, mentions the name of six witches, tried and convicted on one day. Church apologists, writing the story of the witchcraft craze, try to minimize the number hung during the year 1692.

After the hanging of Sarah Good, and the death in jail of the accused Sarah Osburn, the next case that is recorded is that of Bridget Bishop. Her trial was held the first week in June, 1692. Her Irish name alone was enough to condemn her in the sight of English Puritans. She was convicted on short ceremony, and hanged on June 10.

The judges and juries in those days always looked to the preachers for advice, and the court that started by sentencing Bridget Bishop to be hung, and nobody knows how many more, requested divine assistance from the church. The Rev. Cotton Mather was chosen for the purpose. He furnished an inspired opinion in which he said:

> "We judge that, in the prosecution of these and all such witchcrafts there is need of a very critical and exquisite caution, lest by too much credulity for things received only upon the Devil's authority, there be

a door opened for a long train of miserable consequences, and Satan get an advantage over us; for we should not be ignorant of his devices."

Cotton didn't want any of them to get away.

Further on this doctor of divinity says that "it is an undoubted and notorious thing, that a demon may, by God's permission, appear, even to ill purposes, in the shape of an innocent, yea, and a virtuous man."

From this it seems that Jehovah permits Satan— even helps him— to perform his sorceries, so that he— Jehovah—can have the fun of seeing some poor victim hung or burned and sent to Hell.

In conclusion Cotton Mather recommends "the speedy and vigorous prosecutions of such as have rendered themselves obnoxious, according to the directions given in the laws of God and the wholesome statutes of the English nation for the detection of witchcrafts."

Is it to be wondered at that the clerical progeny of these Puritan preachers are to this day the supporters of the warlords?

Is there any infamy that they and their Bible do not endorse?

After prayerfully reading Cotton Mather's bloodthirsty "opinion" the court got busy. It convicted, as being witches of Satan, according to records still extant, Sarah Wildes, Elizabeth Howe, Susanna Martin, Rebecca Nurse, and Sarah Good, already referred to. These were hanged to the glory of the god that inspired the Holy Bible injunction, "Thou shalt not suffer a witch to live," on Tuesday, July 19, 1692. The court then adjourned until the first week in August, when it tried and convicted the following: Martha Carrier, accused of witchcraft; the Rev. George Burroughs, John Procter, George Jacobs, and John Willard. These men were all accused of being in the employ of Satan, or worshiping Jehovah the wrong way, or some such religious offense. They, together with Martha Carrier, were hanged on August 19, 1692.

The evidence is that they had incurred the displeasure of the preachers, and that this was their only crime.

The charges against George Burroughs, a former preacher, but who, it seems, was too decent a man to make good in the superstition business and had taken up other pursuits, claim that he could pick up a barrel of molasses and walk off with it. As no other preacher could be found strong enough to do this, no matter how much he prayed to God for strength, the conclusion was that Burroughs accomplished the feat with Satan's help. Both Cotton and Increase Mather testified that Burroughs was a bad character, and ought to die.[i]

But probably the strongest evidence of his being a tool of Satan that was brought up against him was that he had quit partaking of the "holy communion." We read in the record of his examination as follows: "Being asked when he partook of the Lord's supper, he being (as he said) in full communion at Roxbury, he answered it was so long since he could not tell, yet he owned he was at a meeting one Sabbath at Boston, part of the day, and the other at Charlestown part of a Sabbath when the sacrament happened to be at both, yet did not partake of either. He denied that his house at Casco was haunted yet he owned there were toads."

What more evidence was needed to prove that Satan was getting control of the accused?

He had quit preaching the Calvinist creed; he had begun to doubt the saving grace of dining on the flesh and blood of a sacrificed god; he even doubted that the existence of toads about his premises was an indication that Satan was in the neighborhood. The Rev. George Burroughs had begun to think, and thinking is against the teachings of all orthodox religion. So the Christian powers that be dragged George Burroughs to the scaffold, just as today the same powers drag your boys to slaughter in their profit-making wars. Robert Calef, a Christian of undoubted faith, in a book of the period

---

i   *Wonders of the Invisible World*, by Cotton Mather.

called "More Wonders," says that Burroughs was "carried in a cart with the others (condemned to be hanged) through the streets of Salem to execution. When he was upon the ladder he made a speech for the clearing of his innocency with such solemn and serious expressions as were to the admiration of all present."

We are told that many present wanted to stop the execution. But a holy man of God stepped forth and with his Bible injunctions awed the simple believers. It was Cotton Mather, Jehovah's leading lunatic of New England. Cotton told the assemblage that Buroughs' innocent appearance, his convincing words, his past record as an honest man, were the deceptions of Satan. The toads in his dooryard proved his guilt, just as the juggleries told in the Bible prove its inspiration, or the silk hat on a plutocrat proves his right to exploit the workers. We read in the book quoted, "More Wonders," that "Mr. Cotton Mather, being mounted upon a horse, addressed himself to the people, partly to declare that he (Burroughs) was no ordained preacher, and partly to possess the people of his guilt saying that the Devil has often been transformed into an angel of light; and this somewhat appeased the people and the execution went on."

When it was all over the Christians present exhibited the same instincts that still possess them as they pray to their god for victory on the bloody battlefields. "When he was cut down," so the record runs, "he was dragged by the halter to a hole, or grave, between the rocks, about two feet deep, his shirt and breeches being pulled off, and an old pair of trowsers of one executed put on his lower parts. He was so put in together with Willard and Carrier that one of his hands and his chin, and a foot of one of them, was left uncovered."

On August 5, 1692, John Procter and his wife Elizabeth, residents of Salem, were brought to trial on the charge of both being under the sorceries of Satan. Doubtless some preacher, inspired with the jimjams caused by believing the Book of Revelations, had seen John Procter sitting on his front porch at midnight, watching Satan transform his wife Elizabeth into a wildcat.

Why not?

Massachusetts Under the Rein of the Doctors of Delusion

Did not the author of Revelations see a god with brass feet prowling about with seven stars in his fist and a two-edged sword in his jaws?

Why, then, shouldn't a Puritan preacher also see things?

Anyway, we read that John Bailey, one of the principal witnesses against the Procters, evidently suffering from an attack of indigestion, testified that "on the 25th of May last myself and wife being bound to Boston on the road, when I came in sight of the house where John Procter did live there was a very hard blow struck on my breast, which caused great pain in my stomach and amazement in my head, but did see no person near me only my wife on my horse behind me on the same horse; and when I came against said Procter's house, according to my understanding, I did see John Procter and his wife at said house. Procter himself looked out of the window, and his wife did stand just without the door. I told my wife of it; and she did look that way and see nothing but a little maid at the door. Afterwards, about a mile from the aforesaid house, I was taken speechless for some short time. My wife did ask me several questions, and desired me if I could not speak I should hold up my hand; which I did and immediately I could speak as well as ever. And we came to the way where Salem road cometh into Ipswich road, there I received another blow on my breast, which caused me so much pain I could not sit on my horse. And when I did alight off my horse, to my understanding, I saw a woman coming towards us about 16 or 20 pole from us, but did not know who it was. My wife could not see her. When I did get up on my horse again, to my understanding, there stood a cow where I saw the woman."[i]

Who will say that the days of miracles are over, or that John Bailey, his brain filled with superstition, and, perchance, a considerable quantity of New England rum in his stomach, did not have visions as wonderful as those witnessed by the inspired saint of Patmos?

---

i   Winfield S. Nevins, *Witchcraft in Salem Village*

That, so the records of the period state, Procter and his wife were in jail in Boston when John Bailey rode by his house, with gripes in his insides, and saw John Procter looking out the window and his wife standing by the door, and finally, after dismounting from his horse on account of pains and amazement in his head, saw a woman change into a cow, only makes the affair, from a theological standpoint, all the more marvelous.

John Procter was convicted of being one of Satan's wizards and was hung. His wife Elizabeth escaped on account of her being pregnant. The doctors of divinity could find no Biblical injunction regarding the disposition of a witch caught in that condition. Jehovah had either overlooked the matter, or had left it to the discretion of his saints. So they gave Elizabeth Procter, for the time being at least, the benefit of the doubt, trusting in Jehovah's mercy if they had made a mistake.

However, no sooner had she been safely delivered of her child, than the religious convictions of the Puritans again asserted themselves, and her execution, early in the year 1693, was ordered. But Gov. Phips, after carefully searching the Scriptures, and having taken the matter under prayerful consideration, granted the woman a reprieve, and so Elizabeth Proctor was not hung. The thrifty Puritans took consolation in the fact that, had she been hung, the expense of raising the child would have fallen upon the community. They had already pocketed all there was in sight in the Procter case. We read: "Elizabeth Procter escaped by pleading pregnancy. Some months after the death of her husband she gave birth to a child. Her home had been desolated. Not only had her husband been hanged, three of her children imprisoned, and she herself brought within the very shadow of the gallows, but the officers of the law had stripped that horne of all its worldly possessions."[i]

---

i   Winfield S. Nevins, *Witchcraft in Salem Village*

As confiscation of the property of the condemned formed part of the witchcraft proceedings, it will be noted that witchcraft, like war, was not only a religious, but also a profitable craze.

On the date of the wholesale hangings (August 19, 1692), Judge Samuel Sewall, of Boston, who, together with Nathaniel Saltonstall, Bartholomew Gedney, John Hawthorne, Jonathan Corwin, John Richards, Wait Winthrop and Peter Sargent, was associate with Chief Justice Stoughton in the witch cases narrated, wrote: "This day George Burroughs, John Willard, John Procter, Martha Carrier and George Jacobs were executed at Salem, a very great number of spectators being present. Mr. Cotton Mather was there, Mr. Sims, Hale, Noyes, Cheever etc. All of them said they were innocent, Carrier and all. Mr. Mather said they all died by a Righteous Sentence. Mr. Burroughs by his Speech, Prayer, presentation of his Innocence did much move unthinking persons, which occasions their speaking hardly concerning his being executed."

Outside of the twentieth century massacre at Ludlow it was one of the most religious killings ever pulled off by Christians. At Ludlow Elizabeth Procter would not have escaped on account of her unborn child. Women in her condition were there shot to death and their bodies burned on a pile of oil-soaked railroad ties by gunmen in the employ of one of America's leading Christians.

After the hangings of Friday, August 19, 1692, the court appointed by Gov. Phips convicted and sent to the gallows four more alleged witches—Martha Corey, Mary Easty, Alice Parker and Ann Pudeator. It was a hurry-up job, as the hangings of these victims of the Word of God took place the Monday following, on August 22.

The holy Sabbath was sandwiched in between the two hangings in order to prepare the souls of the saints to solemnly contemplate the carrying out of their god's command.

Also several thousand dollars were confiscated from the condemned and thankfully appropriated by the religious and legal prosecutors.

Two other women charged with witchcraft, Dorcas Hoar and Mary Bradbury, were tried at the same time as those executed on August 22, but were not hanged. Dorcas Hoar was saved from the gallows for the reason that, on the eve of the day appointed for her execution, she confessed to being a witch. She was the first one of whom there is any record of having confessed. This seems to have touched the tender hearts of the Puritans. It also strengthened their faith in the inspired Scriptures.

The sparing of the life of Dorcas Hoar, on account of her confessing to an impossible crime, is a rare instance of the mercy and charity of the Puritans. Judge Samuel Sewall, hearing of the confession, wrote regarding the case: "A petition is sent to town in behalf of Dorcas Hoar who now confesses. Accordingly an order is sent to the sheriff to forbear her execution notwithstanding her being in the warrant to die tomorrow. This is the first condemned person who has confessed."[i]

Thereupon she was left in jail for further developments. It seems uncertain as to what finally became of her. We read: "She (Dorcas Hoar) escaped from jail in the same mysterious manner that so many other of the accused did. These escapes were numerous during the witchcraft trials. Whether the jails were weakly constructed, or the jailers did not guard the prisoners closely at all times, it is not possible to say. It is possible that high officials sometimes connived at the escape of accused persons."[ii]

It is also possible that those who made their escape were penniless, that they had no property to confiscate— not even enough to help pay for the rope to hang them. If there were any officials of that period humane enough to help them escape they must have been men somewhat shaky in their religious convictions.

The other woman, Mary Bradbury, who was tried and convicted of witchcraft, but who was not executed, made no confession, so far

---

i   Sewall Papers
ii   Winfield S. Nevins, *Witchcraft in Salem Village*

as the records disclose. Her escape from the gallows is somewhat mystifying. One writer thinks that "powerful influences were brought to bear to secure her pardon." Perhaps she had well-to-do friends, who put up more money for her pardon than could have been obtained by confiscating the Bradbury estate if she had been hanged. There is nothing in Christian society like the jingle of gold dollars to influence the conceptions of justice. There was certainly evidence enough submitted to hang Mary Bradbury. In the first place she was an old woman along towards fourscore years, just the time of life, according to the most reliable religious authority, both as found in the Scriptures and as testified to by the saints, when Satan delights in turning them into some fierce animal, or mount them on the back of a gander, or a broomstick, and so sail away to a witches' prayer meeting held in the wild recesses of some dizzy mountain ravine.

In the dead of a stormy night, as the lightning flashed a sudden streak across the dismal darkness, and the thunder roared as even did Jehovah once on Sinai, the Puritan, on his knees in prayer, clasping his Bible as superstitiously as does an exploited worker the political party ticket of his exploiters, would catch a terrifying glimpse of the storm-lit skies, and see in rushing clouds and flashing shapes the phantom forms of every old and toothless woman in the neighborhood, flying through space on wings of Hell to the crags and chasms where demons held their infernal communions. Mary Bradbury, in the minds of the saints of Salem, had doubtless taken, time and again, such mad midnight trips.

One of the evidences of witchcraft brought against Mary Bradbury was the testimony of one James Carr, a firm believer in the Bible, as is seen in his testimony. After telling of visits to the Bradbury home this witness declared that he "was taken after a strange manner as if living creatures did run about every part of my body ready to tear me to pieces."

James Carr apparently not only had bugs in his head, but also all over his hide.

In this condition, he declares, he "continued for about three quarters of a year, by times, and I applied myself to Dr. Crosby, who gave me a great deal of physic but could make none work. Though he steeped tobacco in bosset drink he could make none to work; whereupon he told me that he believed I was behaged. And I told him I had thought so a good while. And he asked me by whom, and I told him I did not care for speaking, for one was counted an honest woman, but he urging me I told him, and he said he believed that Mrs. Bradbury was a great deal worse than Good Martin."

The drug doctor then consulted with the divine doctor, and prayers for Carr were added to the prescription. Jehovah heard the prayers, and "one night, something like a cat came to Carr in bed. He went to strike it off but could not move hand or foot for a while."

Jehovah was holding him by the hands and feet while Satan was monkeying with the cat.

Unable to hit the cat, Carr said his prayers; whereupon, we are told, "he did hit it and since then physic had worked on him."

Another member of the Carr family, by the name of Richard, testified as follows: "About thirteen years ago, presently after some difference had happened to be between my honored father, Mr. George Carr, and Mrs. Bradbury, the prisoner at the bar, upon a Sabbath at noon, as we were riding home, by the house of Capt. Thomas Bradbury, I saw Mrs. Bradbury go into her gate, turn the corner of, and immediately there darted out of her gate a blue boar, and darted at my father's horse's legs, which made him stumble, but I saw it no more. And my father said, 'boys, what do you see?' We both answered, 'a blue boar.'"

Satan transformed Mrs. Bradbury into a cat or a blue boar to suit the occasion.

Notwithstanding all this evidence Mrs. Bradbury was not hanged. "Powerful influences," we are told, saved her from the gallows.

During the week following the August 22d hangings, nine servants of Satan were convicted and hanged in Salem: Margaret Scott, Wilmot Reed, Samuel Ward-well, Mary Parker, Abigail Faulkner,

Rebecca Eames, Mary Lacey, Ann Foster and Abigail Hobbs. These constitute, so far as there is any record, the last persons hanged for witchcraft in New England. At this hanging the Rev. Mr. Noyes, preacher of the First Church in Salem, who stood by the gallows and witnessed the executions, piously remarked: "What a sad thing it is to see these firebrands of Hell hanging there."

There were a number of others convicted and sentenced to be hanged at this trial, but who escaped death by confessing that they were under the control of Satan.

Gov. Hutchinson, in his History of Massachusetts, says of this trial: "Those who were condemned and not executed, I suppose all confessed their guilt. I have seen the confessions of several of them."

The swift conviction and execution of those charged with witchcraft, and the chance of escape from death upon confession of being a witch that the kindhearted Christians had provided, made these confessions very popular.

Finally the Governor issued a proclamation "to put an end to witchcraft prosecutions." This was not done, according to the evidence of the period, because the Puritan preachers and others prominent in the church had lost faith in their religion, but because the common people— the children of Satan—began to show signs of revolt against the Christian infamies. We read:

> "Thirteen women and six men were hanged, and one infirm old man, Giles Corey, eighty-one years of age, was pressed to death under a board loaded with heavy weights until his tongue protruded from his mouth and his breath was literally crushed out of him. The society in and about Salem was greatly demoralized by these villainous charges. None was safe. Every person was liable to fall under these accusing girls and their confidential advisers, who had not a little influence over them. A reign of terror existed in the community. The witch trials held in a church in Salem were the all-absorbing matters of interest.

To avoid this cruel persecution many were forced to leave their homes, some going to Europe and some to other localities. The state of society was utterly demoralized" (Blue Laws of Connecticut).

"The evils of this epidemic cast their shadow over a broad surface and darkened the condition of generations. * * * The fields were neglected, fences, roads, barns, even the meeting-house went into disrepair. * * * Scarcity of provisions, nearly amounting to a famine, continued for some time; farms were brought under mortgage or sacrificed, and large numbers of people were dispersed. One locality in Salem village * * * bears to this day the marks of the blight. * * * The ruinous results were not confined to the village, but spread more or less over the country."[i]

The case of Giles Corey forms one of the most brutal pages in Christian history. The torturers and murderers of this old man imitated the savagery of their Bible god to the best of their ability. The following historic description of the affair should be taught in the history classes of our public schools:

"Giles Corey's case was a hard one. He was a sufferer under High Priest Parris and his female accusers. His wife had been complained of, and he knowing her innocence, spoke strongly in her defense. He was arraigned before the same court, but could not be induced to make a plea either of guilty or not guilty. He was a man of some property and he wished what he had to go to his children. He knew that if he confessed or pleaded guilty, his effects, in case of conviction, instead of going to his heirs would be grabbed either by the church or the court that convicted him. He adhered to his resolution, confessing noth-

---

i   C. W. Upham in *Salem Witchcraft*

ing, and making no plea though three times brought before the legal dignitaries. In consequence of the silence he maintained, the sentence of *peine forte et dure,* from the code of King James I, was passed upon him, which was that he be remanded to his low, damp dungeon, to be there laid upon his back on the bare floor, naked for the most part, a board to be laid upon him, and weights enough piled upon the board to nearly crush the life out of him, and to have no sustenance, save on the first day three morsels of very poor bread, and on the second day three draughts of standing or stagnant water, the nearest to be found to the prison door, and this to be alternately his daily diet until he died.

"This horrible sentence was carried out and the suffering that man passed through cannot be conceived. The agony of him who died upon the cross after three hours of exposure was trifling compared with the protracted agony endured by the aged Giles Corey, more than four score years old. It is said the last act in this diabolical tragedy was enacted in an open field near the prison. The wretched sufferer begged his executioners to increase the weights which were crushing him that his agonies might be ended. The hope, however, that he would yield and acknowledge his guilt, so that his property could be secured, induced them not to hurry his death. But he assured them that it was of no use to expect him to yield; that there could be but one way of ending the matter, and that they might as well pile on the rocks and have the matter ended. Calef says that as his body yielded to the pressure, his tongue protruded from his mouth, and an official forced it back with his cane. This inhuman act is attributed to the pious Parris, who made himself so officious in the Salem trials and executions. Upham, in narrating this horrid cruelty, says: 'For a person more than eighty-one years of age this must be allowed to have been a marvelous exhibition of prowess; illustrating, as strongly as anything in human history, the power of a resolute will over the utmost pain and agony of the body and demonstrating that Giles Corey was a man of heroic nerve and a spirit that could not be subdued. This was a case of Christian persecution, where the recipient was, as has been the case in thousands of other instances, vastly superior, in everything that constitutes manhood, to the person who inflicted it.'"[i]

The outraged masses—inspired by Satan—began to conspire against Jehovah's saints. They, too, made accusations of witchcraft; but those they accused were not old and helpless women, and men of doubtful religious convictions, but the very salt of the church. They concluded that a holy law that was good for the goose was good for the gander. As one writer puts it, they found that the only "way to prevent an accusation was to become an accuser." Satan's sinners got as busy as Jehovah's saints in running down witches. The wives of the preachers and leading lights of the church were accused of witchcraft. Satan fought Jehovah with his own weapons. He paraded Jehovah's laws with all the assurance of a devoted believer. The jails became filled with as many Christians as there were heretics. Jehovah and Satan were both at it hammer and tongs. Saints and sinners, in order to escape the penalty, alike confessed. Of this period we read:

> "In this stage of things, such a great accession being made to the ranks of the confessing witches, the power of the delusion became irresistibly strengthened. Mr. Dudley Bradstreet, the magistrate of the place, after having committed about forty persons to jail, concluded he had done enough, and declined to arrest any more. The consequence was that he and his wife were cried out upon, and they had to fly for their lives. They accused his brother, John Bradstreet, with having 'afflicted' a dog. Bradstreet escaped by flight. The dog was executed. The number of persons who had publicly confessed that they had entered

---

[i] *Blue Laws of Connecticut*

into a league with Satan, and exercised the diabolical powers thus acquired to the injury, torment, and death of innocent parties, produced a profound effect upon the public mind. At the same time the accusers had everywhere increased in number, owing to the inflamed state of imagination universally prevalent, which ascribed all ailments or diseases to the agency of witches, to a mere love of notoriety and a passion for general sympathy, to a desire to be secure against the charge of bewitching others, or to a malicious disposition to wreak vengeance upon enemies. The prisons in Salem, Ipswich, Boston, and Cambridge were crowded. All the securities of society were dissolved. Every man's life was at the mercy of every other man. Fear sat on every countenance, terror and distress were in all hearts; silence pervaded the streets; all who could, quit the country; business was at a standstill; a conviction sank into the minds of men that a dark and infernal confederacy had got a foothold in the land, threatening to overthrow and extirpate religion and morality, and establish the Kingdom of the Prince of Darkness in a country which had been dedicated, by the prayers and tears and sufferings of its pious fathers, to the church of Christ, and the service and worship of the true God. The feeling, dismal and horrible indeed, became general that the providence of God was removed from them; that Satan was let loose and that he and his confederates had free and unrestrained power to go to and fro, torturing and destroying whomever he willed. We cannot, by any extent of research or power of imagination, enter fully into the ideas of the people of that day; and it is therefore absolutely impossible to appreciate the awful condition of the community at the point of time to which our narrative has led us."[i]

It is generally conceded by those who have made a study of the history of Salem witchcraft that the accusation of witchcraft made

---

[i] Upham's *Salem Witchcraft*, quoted in *Blue Laws of Connecticut*

against Mrs. Hale, wife of the Rev. John Hale, of Beverly, Mass., one of the most prominent Puritan preachers and associate of Cotton Mather, was the direct and final cause of ending the witchcraft craze. As Upham states, it was what finally broke the spell. Satan, by having a preacher's wife charged with being under his sorceries, had given Jehovah a knock-out blow.

11. From the Beast to the Human

"Man" says J. Howard Moore, "is a talkative and religious ape."[i]

He still follows phantoms—phantoms formed in the brain of the jungle-world.

"What compassion," says Ralph Waldo Emerson, "do these imprisoning forms awaken! You may sometimes catch the glance of a dog which lays a kind of a claim to sympathy and brotherhood. What! somewhat of me down there? Does he know it? Can he, too, as I, go out of himself, see himself, perceive relations? * * * It was in this glance that Ovid got the hint of his metamorphosis; Calidasa of his transmigration of souls. For these fables are our own thoughts carried out. What keeps these wild tales in circulation for thousands of years? What but the wild fact to which they suggest some approximation of theory! Nor is the fact quite solitary, for in varieties of our own species where organization seems to predominate over the genius of man, in Kalmuck or Malay or Flathead Indian, we are sometimes pained by the same feeling; and sometimes, too, the sharp-witted prosperous white man awakens to it. In a mixed assembly we have chanced to see not only a glance at Abdiel so grand and keen, but also in other faces the features of the mink, of the bull, of the rat, and the barn-door fowl."

In the evolution of the race the human is not as yet fully developed. The super-man is on the way.

"Let us label beings by what they are," says Moore, "by the souls that are in them and the deeds they do—not by their color, which is

---

[i] J. Howard Moore, *Universal Kinship*, 1908

pigment, nor by their composition, which is clay. There are philanthropists in feathers and patricians in fur, just as there are cannibals in the pulpit and saurians among the money-changers."[i]

"An anaconda," writes Prentice Mulford, "is but the faint spark of intelligence only awakened into desire to swallow and digest."

Thus have numerous students of biology linked the fables and mythologies, the superstitions and alleged sorceries, the stories of half-men and half-animal, the legends of fairies and nymphs and elves, of gorgons and goblins, with the lingering race memory of our animal ancestry. In the younger world, and among primitive people, these fairy stories generally formed an innocent, and often beautiful, folklore. What is more sweet than some of the fairy tales told in those neglected spots of Ireland, where the Christian's civilization, and his religion, has not entirely effaced the ancient beliefs? Many a child has been lulled to happy dreams as some fond Mother Machree crooned a native song of friendly fairies watching over it as it-slept.

Upon these legends of the younger world, these race-memories of a far-off long ago, the priests of the masterclass—the vulture class—have built a horrible creed. They have turned an innocent dream into a fiendish faith. The fabled goblins of the misty past have been made into avenging gods and frightful devils.

Dead monsters that manured the reptile age have been made immortal deities that ordain exploiters and warlords to rule and rob and murder the people.

When the race reaches sanity it will discover that the gods of the priests, like the governments of the exploiters, are but superstitions. They will find in Nature the only Divinity, the only source of life and sustenance; and they will find in their own errors, their own injustice to their fellow creatures, their own brutal governments and laws, the only Devil.

When the workers of the world become comrades, and the rule and religion of the despoilers are no more, then, and only then, will the race be truly human.

---

i   J. Howard Moore, *Universal Kinship*, 1908

Jehovah's damnation and Satan's sorceries will vanish from earth when plutocracy and priestcraft go.

There will then be none that require the services of these myths. With no powers that be to be ordained, and no threat of endless torment necessary to hold servants in submission to their masters, Jehovah and Satan will both be out of a job. Nothing but servility, the spawn of superstition, holds them in power. Freedom, the child of Knowledge, will have no use for them.

At the hour of this writing, the darkest in history, the predatory powers that be have hurled the race into the depths of their fabled Hell. In the name of their social system and religion they have reddened the earth with blood. In doing so, unless all signs fail, they have pronounced their own doom. Deeper down than once, they say, fell Satan and his hosts from high Heaven's walls, shall fall the social system, and the religion that sustains it, that has brought this insane holocaust upon us. Nor will that social system ever raise its horrid head again. Slowly perhaps, but surely, the people alone will come out of the depths of Hell, and they will leave behind them, forever buried out of sight or chance of resurrection, the rulers and robbers, the gods and goblins, that have ravished and ruined them. The miseries of the exploiting classes, ordained of their god, will never be endured again by men baptized in fratricidal blood. The "ghost of the past" shall depart to darken the earth no more; the "spirit of the future" arises from the agony and ashes! The soul of Humanity shall ride victorious above the raging storm of the ages, over all the thrones and altars, over all the gods and devils of earth. They shall,

> "Lowly, faithful, banish fear,
> Right onward drive unharmed;
> The port, well worth the cruise, is near,
> And every wave is charmed."[i]

---

i   Ralph Wald Emerson's "Terminus"

THE END.

Works by

Tichenor's Books and Pamphlets

The Evils of Capitalism - A Reply to W. F. Lemmons' book, "The Evils of Socialism," 35p., The National Rip-Saw Publ Co, 1912.

Woman Under Capitalism, 32 p., National Rip-Saw Pub. Co, 1912.

The Roman Religion: A Short History of How the Holy Humbug was Hatched, 64 p., Melting Pot, 1913.

Rhymes from the Revloution, 68p., National Rip Saw Pulb., 1914.

The Life and Exploits of Jehovah, 224 p., Phil Wagner Publ, St. Louis, MO., 1915.

The Creed of Constantine; or the world needs a new religion, 189p., Phil Wagner, St. Louis. 1916.

The Sorceries and Scandals of Satan, 177 p., Phil. Wagner Publ, 1917.

Tales of Theology, Jehovah, Satan and the Christian creed, 580 p., The Melting Pot Publ Co, 1918.

The Dictatorship of the Profiteering Class, 28 p., Melting Pot Pub. Co, 1919.

Mythologies, A Materialistic Interpretation : Analyzing the class character of religion, 198 p., The Melting Pot Pub. Co., 1919.

Henry M. Tichenor

Tichenor's Pamphlets for Haldeman-Julius
(At least 24 titles from 1920 to 1923)

Paine, Thomas. *The Age of Reason*. Condensed by H.M. Tichenor, No. 4, 1920
Dumas, Alexander. *Crimes of the Borgias*. Ed. H.M. Tichenor, No. 66. 1922
Church History, No. 67. 1921.
Life of Madame DuBarry, No. 123. 1922
The Theory of Reincarnation Explained, No. 124. 1922
Biology and Spiritual Philosophy, No. 140A.1922
Chinese Philosophy of Life, No 153, 1922
Voices from the Past, No. 169B, 1921
Constantine and the Beginnings of Christianity, No. 170B, 1922
Life of Jack London, No. 183. 1923.
Primitive Beliefs, No. 184. 1921.
Satan and the Saints, No. 201. 1921
Survival of the Fittest, No. 202. 1921
Sun Worship and Later Beliefs, No. 204. 1921
When the Puritans Were in Power, No. 286.
The Olympian Gods. No. 207. 1921
Machiavelli, [Niccolo]. *The Prince*. Ed. H.M. Tichenor. No. 320. 1922.
The Buddhist Philosophy of Life. No. 322. 1922
The Life of Joan of Arc. No. 323. 1922
A Guide to Emerson. No. 338. 1923
Renan, Ernest. *Life of Jesus*. Ed. H.M. Tichenor. No. 340. 1923
Life of Columbus. No. 343. 1923.
Irish Fairy Tales, No. 397, 1923
Irish Folk Songs and Tales. Ed. H.M. Tichenor. No. 398. 1923.

Notes:

Printed in Great Britain
by Amazon.co.uk, Ltd.,
Marston Gate.